신학영어
교본

모든 인간은 하나님의 형상을 닮은 존엄한 존재입니다. 전 세계의 모든 사람들은 인종, 민족, 피부색, 문화, 언어에 관계없이 존귀합니다. 예영커뮤니케이션은 이러한 정신에 근거해 모든 인간이 존귀한 삶을 사는 데 필요한 지식과 문화를 예수 그리스도의 사랑으로 보급함으로써 우리가 속한 사회에 기여하고자 합니다.

신학영어교본

초판 1쇄 찍은 날 · 2006년 9월 8일 | 초판 1쇄 펴낸 날 · 2006년 9월 15일

엮은이 · 김은철 | 펴낸이 · 김승태

편집장 · 김은주 | 편집 · 이덕희, 정은주, 권희중 | 디자인 · 이훈혜, 노지현
영업 · 변미영, 장완철 | 물류 · 조용환
드림빌더스 · 고종원, 이민지 | 홍보 · 설지원

등록번호 · 제2-1349호(1992. 3. 31.) | 펴낸 곳 · 예영커뮤니케이션
주소 · (110-616) 서울 광화문우체국 사서함 1661호 | 홈페이지 www.jeyoung.com
출판사업부 · T. (02)766-8931 F. (02)766-8934 e-mail: jeyoungedit@chol.com
출판유통사업부 · T. (02)766-7912 F. (02)766-8934 e-mail: jeyoung@chol.com

ISBN 89-8350-407-2 (03230)

값 8,000원

■ 잘못 만들어진 책은 교환해 드립니다.

신학영어교본
Reading theological texts in English

김은철 엮음

머리말

수준 있는 영어독해력을 갖는 것은 신학을 연구하고자 하는 사람들에게 필수 조건입니다. 왜냐하면 영국과 미국의 저명한 신학자들이 지금까지 수많은 신학 책들을 출판했고 지금도 계속하고 있기 때문입니다. 또한 국제적인 학술지도 거의 다 영어로 발행하고 있으며 다른 현대언어로 저작한 책들도 영어로 번역하고 있기 때문입니다.

신학을 더 전문적으로 가르치기 위해 신학교에서 신학 영어과목을 개설하고 있습니다. 신학 영어습득을 위해 교과서나 참고서를 발행하여 그 목적을 달성하려고 하는 것입니다. 시중에 출판된 몇 가지의 책들은 나름대로 특징이 있지만 본서는 다른 관심을 가지고 접근했습니다. 다시 말하면, 신학적 논리능력을 배양하기 위해서 편집했습니다. 수집한 논문 요약들은 영국의 우수한 대학의 박사들의 논문입니다. 이것을 읽고 이해하게 되면 다양한 신학적인 용어와 신학 논제의 범위, 논문의 구성, 논문의 전개방법 등을 알게 될 것입니다. 요약들이 짧게 구성되어 있으므로 재미있고 지루하지 않아 학습도를 증진 시킬 것입니다.

주로 성서신학의 논문요약들을 배열했지만, 조직신학,

역사신학, 선교신학에 관한 것들도 할애하여 정리되어 있으므로 폭 넓은 신학을 접할 수 있는 기회가 될 것입니다. 한국은 이미 세계적으로 알려진 기독교 국가가 되었으므로 이제는 세계적인 신학자들이 배출되어야 할 것입니다. 그런 바램으로 이 책을 편집하여 발행했습니다.

예영커뮤니케이션의 김승태 사장님의 변함없는 관심과 배려로 또 하나의 책이 나오게됨에 대하여 심심한 감사를 금할 수 없습니다. 귀 회사의 번창을 기원합니다.

2006. 8. 18.

김은철 박사

Table of Contents

1. Studies in the interpretation of Genesis 26:1-33	12
2. Genesis 38 in the context of the 'Joseph Story'	15
3. The deuteronomistic historian's use of the Transjordan traditions	18
4. Theodicy and the problem of human surrender in Job	20
5. Qoheleth's concept of God	22
6. Early Israelite wisdom	25
7. An examination of kingship and messianic expectation in Isaiah 1-35	27
8. The religion of the landless	30
9. The theology of blessing in the Hebrew scripture	32
10. Discipleship and family ties according to Mark and Matthew	34
11. Matthew's inclusive story	37
12. Matthew's Emmanuel Messiah	40
13. New shepherds for Israel	43
14. Leadership and discipleship: a study of Luke 22:24-30	46
15. Secular and Christian leadership in Corinth	49

16. Power through weakness	52
17. The development of early Christian pneumatoloy with special reference to Luke-Acts	55
18. Eschatology, history and mission in the social experience of Lucan Christians	58
19. Contexts and meanings	61
20. Paul's purpose in writing Romans	64
21. The relationship between theology and ethics in the letter to the Ephesians	67
22. Luke's preface and the synoptic problem	70
23. The Davidic Messiah in Luke-Acts	72
24. The artistry of John	75
25. The prophetic vision of the Son of Man in the Fourth Gospel	78
26. The example and teaching of Jesus in Romans 12:1-15:13	80
27. Monotheism and Christology in 1 Corinthians 8.4-6	82
28. The cross in Corinth	86
29. Obeying the truth: a study of Paul's exhortation in Galatians 5-6	88

30. Paul's language about God	91
31. The use of the Old Testament in the composition of First Peter	93
32. The relationship between worship and suffering in 1 Peter and Revelation	95
33. The genre of the Book of Revelation from a source-critical perspective	97
34. Friendship	99
35. Tertullian's understanding of death and the afterlife	102
36. Creation theology in Origen	104
37. Prayer and miracle in the spirituality of St. Augustine	107
38. St. Augustine of Hippo on Christ, his Church, and the Holy Spirit	110
39. The knowledge and consciousness of Christ in the light of the writings of St John of the Cross	113
40. Social and political aspects of the career of St. Basil of Caesarea	116
41. The Desert Fathers on personal relationships	118
42. Christology and anthropology in the spirituality of Maximus the confessor	121

43. Knowledge, faith and philosophy in Thomas Aquinas	124
44. Incarnation and inspiration	128
45. Faith in the theology of Dietriech Bonhoeffer	131
46. The relationship between revelation and religion in the theology of Karl Barth and his critics	133
47. Human fallenness	136
48. Evangelical theology 1857-1900	139
49. The concept of the vicarious humanity of Christ in the theology of Thomas Forsyth Torrance	142
50. The concept of regeneration in Christian thought	145
51. The Trinity and the contemporary doctrine of God	148
52. The logic and language of the incarnation	150
53. The Holy Spirit and religious experience in Christian literature c.90-200	152
54. The puritan meditative tradition, 1599-1691	155
55. The challenge of transformation	158
56. I am a sort of middle man	161

57. Interdependence of law and grace in 163
    John Wesley's teaching and preaching
58. The purpose of stating the faith 165
59. Jewish mission in the Christian state 168
60. A missionary of the road 171

1 Studies in the interpretation of Genesis 26:1-33
Nicol, G.G. *Oxford*. D.Phil. 1987.

The thesis addresses both literary and historical questions to the Isaac Narrative, and the course it follows is set out in the Introduction. In Chapter One, following the formal definition of the passage to be analysed, the literary structure of Genesis 26:1-33 is examined. This examination reveals a narrative which, although episodic in nature, displays much evidence of unity. The narrative is concerned with the relationship between Isaac and Abimelech, and displays a strong interest in the welfare of the Philistines. The structure of the six episodes which comprise the Isaac narrative are analysed in Chapter Two, and these analyses show how the narrator has been able to portray a steady increase in Isaac's prosperity without thereby adversely affecting Abimelech's. In Chapter Three the perspective of the literary analysis is filled out by an examination of some of the ways in which the patriarchal narratives of Genesis 12-25 impinge on the reading of Genesis 26:1-33. The fact that the Isaac material relates events so similar to those which are narrated in the story of Abraham requires a careful examination of biblical materials, such as the doublets, in order to discriminate among their similarities and their differences. Part One is concluded in Chapter Four with a number of observations on the literary method applied in the preceding chapters.

Part Two is concerned with the interpretation of the Isaac narrative from a historical perspective. Chapter Five introduces the form-critical conclusions of Lutz and Coats, and provides an analysis of the structure and contents of the narrative. To some extent, this reading is informed by the earlier literary reading of Chapter Two, and it results in the identification of a unified composite narrative. Chapter Five continues with a discussion of Noth's traditio-historical arguments concerning the priority of Isaac over Abraham in the tradition, and is concluded with a discussion of the narrative's composition history. Chapter Six provides a survey of all the references to Isaac which occur outside of Genesis. These references, however, provide no firm evidence of an early or independent Isaac tradition and certainly do not preclude the view that Genesis 26:1-33 is a literary revision of a number of Abraham narratives.

A brief concluding chapter reviews the main conclusions of the Thesis and discusses the comparative value of the two styles of biblical study represented by Parts One and Two.

Genesis 38 in the context of the 'Joseph Story'
Golder, M.C. *Manchester*. PhD. 1985.

The present thesis is that Genesis 38 is a carefully constructed narrative, designed to fit into the Joseph Story of Gen. 37-50. Its details reveal many connections with those of the rest of Gen. 37ff. Its presence adds greatly to the appreciation of the problems which beset the family of the Promise as the patriarchal era drew to its close.

To prove this the argument proceeds in three stages.

Section 1 (chs. 1-3) examines Gen. 38's plan and plot in order to show that it is a carefully designed unity built in a ground-plan involving seven sections arranged in a symmetrical ABCA' B' C' A" pattern. The Tale of Judah and Tamer shows how Judah is humiliated for neglecting Tamer's rights, while her giving birth to twins restores his line - placed in jeopardy by the deaths of Er and Onan.

Section 2 (chs. 4-7) studies the text of Gen. 37-50 synchronically in order to show how many connections of theme and vocabulary Gen. 38 has with its context. Their number renders it very unlikely that Gen. 38 is an interpolation which is only vaguely connected with the Joseph Story. Gen. 37ff. concerns God's salvation of his Chosen People and the sibling rivalry of Joseph and his brothers - in particular that between Joseph and Judah. Gen. 38 has an important function within Gen. 37ff. It shows, for example, Judah's punishment for letting Jacob think Joseph was dead; and it enables the narrator to show how Judah was less worthy than Joseph to be the family's next leader and the heir to the Promise made to the patriarchs by God.

Section 3 (chs. 8-11) involves a diachronic

study of Gen. 37ff. It attempts to discover how far the text is a real unity. The careful examination suggests that there are two sets of material within the confines of Gen. 37-50. The first seems to be a unified narrative about Joseph, designed to fit into its present position between the patriarchal narratives and the account of the Exodus. It may have been produced in the 6th or 5th Cents B.C. In this Joseph Story Gen. 38 is not an interpolation, but an integral part of the Story's plan and plot. Gen. 38 fills out the Story's portrait of Judah, the man who tried - but failed - to supplant Joseph as the brothers' future leader. The second seems to be a set of insertions into the Joseph narrative, apparently the work of the Priestly editor of Genesis (late 5th or early 4th Cents B.C). These insertions are intended to add more information about Jacob and his family's descent into Egypt.

3 The deuteronomistic historian's use of the Transjordanian traditions: history and symbol

Chong, E.C.M. London, King's College. Ph.D. 1991.

The pre-exilic deuteronomistic Historian's hope for the restoration of Israel as the people of Yahweh is seen in his symbolic and secondary historiographic use of the Tranjordanian conquest-settlement traditions. Comparing the critical period between the Josinaic reforms and the days immediately after the death of Josiah with the critical moment of Israel's election at the Transjordan (Dt 4.1-14; 7.6-8; 26.15-19; 27.9f), the historian used the Transjordian traditions symbolically. The Transjordan symbolized the proof and guarantee of Yahweh's ability and willingness to fulfill the promised made to the fathers (Dt. 2.26-3.7; 31.3-6; Jos 2.9-11; 9.9f). But this fulfillment was conditioned upon Israel's obedience and willingness to trust Yahweh. The historian saw this proof and offer of guarantee as still standing in his time. It would function as an exhortation for Israel's choice for Yahweh as the only realistic means to its restoration as the people of Yahweh, if Israel would respond to this symbol positively through obedience and trust in Yahweh.

But he saw continuing signs of Israel's apostate behaviour during his time, a characteristic that marked the whole of Israel's relationship with Yahweh both before and after its election. In the event of Israel's failure once again to respond appropriately to this new opportunity for restoration, the Transjordanian will symbolize Yahweh's indictment against and rejection of Israel.

The historian's secondary historiographic use of the Tranjordanian traditions centred on his attempt to restore the tribal status of Manasseh through his creation of a link between the House of Machir son of Ammiel of Lodebar with the tribe Manasseh. This link was achieved by the 'creation' of a Manassite clan with the designation 'Half-tribe Manasseh'.

4 Theodicy and the problem of human surrender in Job

Horne, M.P. *Oxford*. D.Phil. 1989.

This study has as its main concern J. Crenshaw's claim that the ending of the book of Job (Job 42:2-6) advances a theodicy which advocates extreme human surrender to the deity. Crenshaw's conclusions are challenged on the grounds that both his method (the use of the concept of 'anthropodicy'), and the extent of his analysis of the book of Job, are too superficial. When reconsidered, however, one central feature of the book challenges the very nature of such extreme surrender: the book of Job calls attention to the 'false consciousness of reality' created by those religious beliefs which legitimize such surrender. This problem is present in virtually every occurrence of surrender, or the admonition to such surrender, throughout the book - except Job 42:2-6.

In the prologue Job surrenders to God under a 'false consciousness of reality.' This is evident in the contradictory terms which reveal that empirical reality is obscured from Job by his piety. In the dialogue strong challenge is raised against these terms of surrender to God, most immediately by Job in 3:23ff where he questions the 'hidenness of man' s way.' But Job challenges his friends' rationale for surrender by showing that their belief in human inferiority and moral worthlessness is no guarantee of God' s just treatment of humans. Finally, Yahweh responds to Job: first, by insisting that he is indeed limited and inferior and has no choice but to surrender to Yahweh; second, by showing Job that such surrender does not rob humans of their inherent worth and dignity. Thus Job' s surrender and genuine change of mind in 42:2-6 cannot be considered to be offered under a false consciousness of realty, nor is it so extreme as to debase Job to be before God.

5 Qoheleth's concept of God

Heskin, K. *Leeds*. PhD. 1985.

The thesis is presented in three parts:

Part One

A fresh examination of the theological assertions and implications of the Book of Ecclesiastes, treated as the work of one man, is undertaken. God's activity, which - more than His personal attributes - is the subject of Qoheleth's attention, is divided into two categories: endogenous divine activity (arising from within and unaffected by outward stimuli such as human virtue of sinfulness) and reactive divine activity. The former, which is the more prevalent, inevitably highlights God's sovereignty and His superiority to man. Qoheleth's low appraisal of man and the human condition brings the disparity between God and man into even greater relief, and adds to the cold theological atmosphere of the book. A partial counterbalance is provided by acknowledgements of God's reactive and retributive activity.

Part Two

Parallels between the Book of Ecclesiastes and some biblical texts (Job, Prov. and Gen.) are examined. It is suggested that material of the sort which figures in the Book of Job could have furnished Qoheleth with his main theological and anthropological ideas, and that material of the sort which figures in the Book of Proverbs could have acted as a catalyst for some of his ideas. In addition, it is argued that he was significantly influenced by the Book of Genesis (esp. Gen. 2-3).

Part Three

Parallels between the Book of Ecclesiastes and extra-biblical texts from Egypt, Mesopotamia, Ras Shamra and Greece are examined. The only parallels that adduce satisfactory evidence of dependence are those between Ecc. 9:7-9 and the Speech of Siduri from the *Epic of Gilgamesh*. All others lack a sufficiently unusual correspondence of content or form to warrant their being designated as borrowings.

Early Israelite wisdom

Weeks, S.D.E. *Oxford*. D.Phil. 1991.

The thesis is an examination of the wisdom literature preserved in the book of Proverbs, and of evidence pertinent to the nature and historical setting of this material. The first section examines the arrangement of sayings in the sentence literature, reviews the comparative Near Eastern material and its significance for the exegesis of Proverbs, and discusses the claims that early wisdom was secular, rejecting them. The second section concentrates upon the setting of the literature, with studies of 'wisdom' and 'wise men' in the Old Testament, the internal evidence for associating Proverbs with the royal court, the nature of the Joseph narrative, Solomon's wisdom and the influence of Egypt of his administration, and, finally, the biblical and epigraphic evidence for formal education in Israel. On the basis of these studies, it is concluded that conventional views of the wisdom literature as scribal and pedagogical are ill-founded and in need of revision. It is suggested that indications within Proverbs itself are a better guide to the nature of the material, and that early wisdom literature should be viewed as an integral part of the literary culture within Israel, not as the product of an international movement or specific professional group.

An examination of kingship and messianic expectation in Isaiah 1-35

Wehner, P.D. London, *King's College*. PhD. 1990.

This dissertation examines Isa. 7:10-17; 8:23-9:6, 11:1-9 and 32:1-8 to determine Isaiah's contribution to messianic expectation. The writings of the prophet Isaiah were pivotal to the formulation of the concept of Messiah and contain some of the earliest elements which developed into the concept. Previous to Isaiah some of the early psalms presented the king of Israel in an idealised manner, but Isaiah realized that in practical reality the Davidic kings fell far short of these idealised characteristics. This led Isaiah to speak of a coming deliverer of Israel who would fulfill the hopes present in these early psalms.

The first chapter of this dissertation contains a history of messianic interpretation centering upon three time periods in which there were significant changes in the understanding of the Messiah (third century BCE-third century CE; eighteenth- nineteenth centuries CE; and the twentieth century CE). The second chapter contains an exegesis of the messianic passages in Isaiah 1-35. Based on this exegesis, the third chapter summarizes Isaiah's concept of this ideal deliverer and how later authors used Isaiah's understanding to develop the idea of the Messiah.

In particular the third chapter discusses Isaiah's belief in an ideal deliverer who would purify the nation of Israel, lead them victoriously against the Assyrians, and then set up a kingdom characterized by peace and prosperity which would endure forever. The concept of an ideal deliverer was taken up and further developed in other biblical passages. New Testament authors used passages from Isaiah and applied them to Christ. We believe that this is possible for two reasons:

(a) Isaiah presented the core concepts about a future deliverer even though he did not realize how these prophecies would specifically be fulfilled. Since the core was already present, later authors were not re-reading or finding a new meaning in the passages of Isaiah but were using the original meaning and re-applying it to Christ.

(b) We believe that the idea of an ideal deliverer is a pattern which has been expanded and developed. It was begun in the Old Testament and carried on into the New Testament referring to different people and historical situations, but the original intent as expressed in the Old Testament passage(s) remained the same.

8 The religion of the landless: a sociology of the Babylonian exile

Smith, D.L. Oxford. D.Phil. 1985.

In this study, the Babylonian Exile of the Jews is approached from the perspective of a sociological analysis of more recent historical cases of mass deportation and refugee behaviour. After this survey, four behaviour patterns are isolated that function as 'Mechanisms for Survival' for minorities in crisis and under domination in a foreign environment. These 'Mechanisms' includes 1) structural adaptation, 2) the rise of, and conflict between, new leaders, 3) new folklore patterns, especially 'Hero' stories, and 4) adoption or elaboration of ritual as a means of boundary maintenance and identity preservation.

These four mechanisms are then illustrated from Exilic texts of the Old Testament. The rise of Elders and the changing nature of the Bet Abot are seen as structural adaptation. The conflict of Jeremiah and Hananiah, and the advice of Jeremiah in his 'letter', is seen as the conflict of new leaders in crisis. The 'Diaspora

Novella' is compared to Messianic expectation and especially to Suffering Servant to show how folklore can reflect social conditions and serve a function as 'hero stories'. Finally, the latest redactional layers of 'P' reveal concern for purity and separation that expressed itself in social isolationism and boundary maintenance, particularly in the dissolution of marriages with foreign wives. There is also a section on social conflict after the restoration, as a measure of the independent development of exilic social ideology and theology.

The conclusion is that sociological analysis of the Exilic material reveals the exilic-post-exilic community exhibiting features of a minority group under stress, and the creative means by which that group responds by Mechanisms for Survival.

9 The theology of blessing in the Hebrew scriptures

Taylor, J.B. *Open University*. Ph.D. 1992.

This work examines the root [*barakah*] in the Hebrew Scriptures contextually, to determine the content of blessing and to ask what the concept of blessing has to say about the nature and purposes of God. It is examined in the separable strands, in the Yahwist, the Deuteronomists, the Priestly writings, the Historical writers, the Psalms and the Wisdom Literature, and in the Prophets.

The main theological conclusions are that blessing is a way of talking about God immanent in everything he has made. It is his invitation to human beings to cooperate with him in his creative purposes for the world. It is best understood in terms of 'gift', as well as being, in the Priestly writings, the potential for growth and development in every created thing. Blessing is a theological concept which values the material and the physical. It reveals the importance of categories of relationship, presence and community solidarity. God's promise of blessing to Abraham is for the sake of the whole human race. It is concerned with God's abundant provision for the maintenance of life, including his provision for the poor and needy who do not have immediate access to God's bounty. Whereas curse is about exclusion, blessing is about inclusion and identification.

The high expression of a living relationship with God is in worship, in which human beings join with the whole created world to bless God, to praise and glorify him. Within the mutuality of the relationship to which God invites his creation, worship matters to God as well as to his children. Blessing is an eschatological concept which points to the [*barakah*] of the end-time. It has been devalued. The rich tones which it has in the Hebrew scriptures need to be restored to enrich our worship and to enhance our appreciation of the wonder of God's world.

10 Discipleship and family ties according to Mark and Matthew

Barton, S.C. London, *King's College*. PhD. 1992.

From the very beginning, following Jesus or conversation to the Christian way commonly generated intra-familiar tensions. The social impact of conversion was a major concern. Insiders and outsiders alike bear witness to the threat to family and household ties posed by a transfer of the believer's primary allegiance to Christ.

The main aims and structures of the present study are as follows. First, it seeks to show that the demand to subordinate family ties in response to the call to follow Jesus is intelligible in the context of beliefs and practices both in Judaism and in Greco-Roman philosophy of the first century. This is the subject of Chapter One, where attention is given to Philo, Josephus and Qumran, on the Jewish side, and to the Cynics and Stoics, on the Greco-Roman side.

Second, on the basis of a detailed analysis of

the relevant narrative and sayings traditions, the study demonstrates that the implications of discipleship for family ties is a theme of considerable importance in the Gospels of Mark and Matthew, and that such traditions open up a window onto what may properly be called the counter-cultural ethos Marcan and Matthean Christianity. Chapter Two focuses on Mark and Chapter Three on Matthew; and a substantial continuity between the two gospels is established, as well as certain significant differences.

In the analysis of the relevant material in the gospels, an explicitly multidisciplinary approach is taken which combines the traditio-historical disciplines of form- and redaction-criticism with methods which have developed more recently in the interpretation of the gospels: literary criticism and sociological criticism. A third aim of the study, therefore, is to commend this multidisciplinary approach as a way of doing most justice to the nature of the gospels themselves - as historical testimony, as written texts, and as documents shaped by communal concerns.

Matthew's inclusive story: a study in the narrative rhetoric of the gospel and the contribution of redaction criticism to literary studies

Howell, D.B. *Oxford*. D.Phil. 1988.

Telling a story as found in Matthew involves 'narrative rhetoric'; the gospel is constructed in order to influence readers, and literary techniques are used to accomplish this purpose. Matthew has been described as an 'inclusive story' in which the experiences of the evangelist's post-Easter church are contained in the story of Jesus' earthly ministry. The purpose of this thesis is to explore the inclusive nature of Matthew by means of a type of reader-response literary criticism that seeks to describe the literary techniques by which a reader's experience of the text is shaped.

Chapter 1 outlines the presuppositions of the literary paradigm used in the study and discusses the limitations of traditional historical-critical methods in explicating how the gospel's narrative can engage and influence readers. Chapters 3, 4 and 5 form the center of the thesis. Matthew's narrative rhetoric is described by means of a narrative criticism that examines respectively the gospel's story, story-teller, and audience. These chapters are bracketed by two chapters which relate the literary methods used to more traditional methods of biblical interpretation as represented in redaction criticism.

In Chapter 2 previous studies of Matthew which used salvation history as a theological concept able to encompass both the time of Jesus and the time of the church are examined. The contribution of authorial intention to interpreting the gospel's story is explored in chapter 6 by means of redaction criticism since this is the method used in Synoptic studies to infer authorial intention. The thesis is developed that the readers who are included or implied in the story should not simply be identified with the disciples. Discipleship does not mean membership in a character group but concerns the values and norms which the implied author wishes the implied reader to adopt. As the character who is the spokesman for these values and norms, and who embodies the demands of discipleship made in his teaching, Jesus can be seen as the model for discipleship in Matthew.

12 Matthew's Emmanuel Messiah: a paradigm of the presence for God's people

Kupp, D.D. *Durham*. PhD. 1992.

This study begins with the presumption of the wholeness and integrity of Matthew's narrative, and assumes the gospel story to have an inherently dramatic structure which invites readers to inhabit imaginatively its narrative world and respond to its call. But, since we are concerned with the role of both reader and author, this study also assumes a text with an historical author and context.

The introduction focuses on the meta-critical dilemma facing New Testament students - what is the text and how do they read it? - and seeks some balance in terms of Krieger's analogy of the text as both window and mirror. Proposed is a narrative reading of Matthew's presence motif alongside a redaction critical assessment of it.

In Chapter 2 the elements of narrative theory

are introduced and relevant terms defined: the structure of narrative, the function of the narrator, points of view. Chapter 3 becomes an exercise in narrative reading, with Matthew's presence motif providing the focus, and the implied reader's interaction with the story being predominant in interpretation. Characters, rhetorical devices, and points of view are discussed, to understand the motif's development throughout the story's progress.

The thrust of Chapter 4 is thereafter to examine divine presence as a dominant motif within Matthew's most important literary context: the Jewish Patriarchs, the Sinai experience, and the Davidic-Zion traditions are assessed. Chapter 5 follows with a more detailed examination of the OT 'I am with you/God is with us' formula and its μεθυμνημων language, so strongly connected to Matthew's presence motif.

Chapters 6-8 build in these investigations with a closer analysis of the three critical 'presence passages' of Mt 1:23, 18:20 and 28:20. The passages and their contexts are probed from a redaction critical perspective, guided by the narrative investigation of Chapter 3, and the background from Chapters 4 and 5.

The three major 'presence passages' examined in Chapters 6-8 are also complimented by a number of secondary issues: worship, wisdom, the Spirit and the poor in Matthew, and their relation to Jesus' divine presence. These are discussed in Chapter 9. Chapter 10 summarizes and looks briefly at some implications.

New shepherds for Israel: a historical and critical study of Matthew 9:35-11:1

McKnight, S. *Nottingham.* PhD. 1986.

The Gospel of Matthew includes five recognizable discourses and the second of these, known as the Missionary Discourse (Mt 9:35-11:1), has never been investigated with a critical methodology and it is the purpose of this thesis to provide such a study.

Though other angles could shed light, the most illuminating historical context of this discourse is Matthew's constant interaction with the Pharisees and the latter are viewed from four angles: they are depicted as (1) nomistic in orientation, (2) politically-concerned and influential, (3) the theological guardians of the traditions of Israel, and (4) those who oppose both Jesus and his followers.

In order to understand Matthew's redactional concerns, one must first separate as clearly as possible the traditions from the redaction. Matthew composes, rather than creates, his discourse largely on the basis of Markan, Q and M traditions, many of which were originally given in different contexts, but the author carefully redacts each tradition throughout in order to present his own theology.

Particular theological perspectives emerge clearly from a redaction-critical analysis of the second discourse. Matthew, by shaping and interpreting the traditions, presents the mission of the Twelve as Jesus' replacement of the Pharisees with the Twelve as the New Shepherds for Israel. Furthermore, as Matthew looks inward, at his own church in shaping this discourse, he exhorts the itinerants to take consolation in the fact that both their ministry and fate are the same as the ministry and fate of Jesus.

In conclusion, Matthew transmits Jesus traditions by conservation, expansion and creative interpretation. Furthermore, Matthew's church seems to have been directly opposed by the Pharisaic leaders of Judaism and the dividing line appears to be one of the rightful leadership of Israel. Matthew argues that, due to corrupt leadership, the Pharisees have been rejected and God's Messiah, Jesus, has replaced the Pharisees with the twelve apostles as the New Shepherds of Israel.

14 Leadership and discipleship: a study of Luke 22:24-30
Nelson, P.K. *Bristol*. PhD. 1991.

The aim of the study is to discern the Lukan significance of Luke 22:24-30. Limited scholarly work on the text and the importance of its context and content justify an extended analysis. Background studies of authority patterns (ch.2), table (ch.3) and reversal motifs (ch.4), and the testamentary genre (ch.5) constitute Part One and provide a multi-faceted platform upon which the direct and detailed analysis in Part Two of 22:24-27 (ch.6), 22:28-30 (ch.7) and 22:24-30 as a literary whole (ch.8) is based. The interplay of looking closely and stepping back permitted by this two-part structure facilitates the quest for the text's meaning, as does an emphasis on redaction- and literary-critical priorities.

The work seeks to demonstrate a Lukan unitary conception for 22:24-30, contrary to the orientation of much tradition-critical study. The pericope's unity is evidenced in its overarching, full-circle reversal form (the great are to serve; loyal 'servants' will be 'great') as a pattern for discipleship which increases motivation for perseverance in adversity. Also unifying the texts are a pervasive interest in authority which presents a challenge to conventional ideas of power and greatness (elevation comes to those who lead 'from below'), and a keen concern for the solidarity of the apostles with Jesus during his earthly life and in the eschatological age.

Certain specific assertions of Part Two which undergird the above claims are these: the contrast structure of 22:25-27 with Jesus' self-description as 'the servant' (v.27) paints the apostles' quarrel over greatness (v.24) not as an innocent rivalry but as a sharply negative event, and, despite a recent claim to the contrary, it portrays the kings and benefactors (v.25) as distinctly negative examples: the chief expression of Jesus' servant leadership (v.27) is humble and benefit-giving death; Jesus recalls his 'trials' (v.28) at the time of his public ministry during which the apostles persevered with him; the conferral of kingship and promise of exaltation (vv.29-30) anticipate fulfillment not in the church age but in the eschaton.

Secular and Christian leadership in Corinth: a socio-historical and exegetical study of 1 Corinthians 1-6

Clarke, A.D. *Cambridge*. PhD. 1992.

Many studies of New Testament church leadership this century have suffered from one of two imbalances. They have either been too narrowly constructed on the theological ideals of the Pauline material; or too strongly dictated by modern social theory. A more appropriate method, adopted here with regard to leadership practices in 1 Corinthians 1-6, is to assess the New Testament material in the light of its social and historical background.

Graeco-Roman leadership profiles and practices in first century Roman Corinth (constructed from extant epigraphic, numismatic and literary sources) form the principal primary sources. The ways in which social elites jostled for position and popularity in Graeco-Roman city-life is described from a comprehensive catalogue of first century Corinthian leaders in this Roman colony. The place of status, patronage and benefaction, political enmity and oratory are crucial for a successful profile of secular political leadership in the city.

Evidence is examined which demonstrates that within the Christian community there were some from the Corinthian social elite. Some of these were responsible for undermining Paul's perception of leadership. They elevated the place of worldly wisdom, boasted about status, created divisions over personal loyalties, sought a leadership reliant on persuasive oratory, gave greater defense to significant patrons in the church, and sought to gain greater personal influence by pursuing fellow Christians in the secular law courts.

In the light of this intrusion of secular perceptions of leadership into the Corinthian church, Paul defines for the Corinthians his principles of leadership. This is achieved by giving a decisive critique of secular leadership within the church and a presentation of his principles of Christian leadership. His own example demonstrates an avoidance of persuasive oratory and secular boasting, and a refusal to give particular esteem to certain Christians on the grounds of their secular status.

16 Power through weakness: an historical and exegetical examination of Paul's understanding of the ministry in 2 Corinthians

Savage, T.B. *Cambridge*. PhD.1987.

In 2 Corinthians Paul repeatedly describes his ministry in terms two contradictory, yet overlapping, experiences. His is a vocation of glory through shame (ch. 3), life through death (ch. 4) and power through weakness (chs. 11-13). The aim of this thesis is to make sense of these paradoxes.

In the first part of our study we examine the *background* of the paradoxes. It is suggested that they represent the product of the interaction of two opposing viewpoints: the worldly outlook of Paul's critics and Paul's own Christ-centered perspective. An exegesis of key biblical texts (1 Cor 1:10-4:21; 2 Cor 1:23-2:11; 7:5-16; 10:1-18; 11:6-33; 12:14-18) and a study of the social outlook of first century Corinth - here using the insights of classical archaeology - show that Paul's critics are evaluating him on the basis of the self-exalting standards of their secular environment. Accordingly, they allege that his humility and weakness make a mockery of his claim to be a minister of the glorious gospel of Christ. In response Paul argues that it is precisely his weakness which not only affirms his position in Christ but also ensures that his ministry will be accompanied by divine power.

In the second part of the thesis we consider the *meaning* of this paradox. An exegesis of 2 Cor 3-4 is particularly instructive. Contrary to the accusations of his critics, Paul's gospel is exceedingly glorious. It is brighter than the light which adorned the face of Moses (3:7-11), and represents the fulfillment of the great eschatological light promised in LXX Isaiah (4:6). But as such it is a paradoxical light, manifested preeminently in the person of the crucified Christ (4:6). Those who have eyes to see this light reflect its paradoxical character - they are stamped with the image of the cross, and so manifest glory through shame (3:18). This suggests that, so long as the present evil age lasts (4:3), it is only in the humility of those who have been conformed to Christ that the power and glory of God can be manifested. Paul therefore carries about the dying of Jesus order that the life of Jesus might be manifested (4:10-12).

As a minister of the gospel of Christ Paul has no option but to respond to his critics: 'When I am weak, then I am strong.'

The development of early Christian pneumatology with special reference to Luke-Acts

Menzies, R.P. *Aberdeen*. PhD. 1989.

The author seeks to demonstrate that Paul was the first Christian to attribute soteriological functions to the Spirit and that this original element of Paul's pneumatology did not influence wider (non-Pauline) sectors of the early church until after the writing of Luke-Acts. Three interrelated arguments are offered in support of his thesis.

In Part One he argues that soteriological functions were generally not attributed to the Spirit in inter-testamental Judaism. The Spirit was regarded as the source of prophetic inspiration, a *donum superadditum* granted to various individuals so they might fulfill a divinely appointed task. The only significant exceptions to this perspective are found in later sapiential writings. (1QH, Wisd).

In Part Two he argues that Luke, influenced

by the dominant Jewish perception, consistently portrays the gift of the Spirit as a prophetic endowment which enables its recipient to participate effectively in the mission of God. Although the primitive church, following in Jesus' footsteps, broadened the functions traditionally ascribed to the Spirit in first-century Judaism and thus presented the Spirit as the source of miracle-working power (as well as prophetic inspiration), Luke resisted this innovation. For Luke the Spirit remained the source of special insight and inspired speech. The important corollary is that neither Luke nor the primitive church attributes soteriological significance to the pneumatic gift in a manner analogues to Paul.

In Part Three he argues, on the basis of his analysis of relevant Pauline texts, that the early Christian traditions used by Paul do not attribute soteriological functions to the Spirit, and that sapiential traditions from the Hellenistic Jewish milieu which produced Wisdom provided the conceptual framework for Paul's distinctive thought. Thus he maintains there were no Christian precursors to Paul at this point and that Paul's perspective represents an independent development.

18

Eschatology, history and mission in the social experience of Lucan Christians: a sociological study of the relationship between ideas and social realities in Luke-Acts

Martin, T.W. *Oxford*. D.Phil. 1986.

The subject of this thesis is the relationship between eschatology and history in the Christian community for which Luke-Acts was written.

Chapter 1 formulates the problem in terms of Luke's eschatology. It argues that Luke and his community thought of the End as 'near' and that Luke's historical perspective affected his eschatology. Luke-Acts represents a community that held a relevant eschatological hope and was aware of continuing history. This is the interpretive problem this thesis seeks to enlighten. The perspective to be used in approaching this problem is that of sociological analysis. Chapter 2 explores the use of sociological perspectives in New Testament study and the benefits to be achieved by the use of the sociology of knowledge. Chapter 3 is a sociological analysis of the community in terms of date, location, stratification, racial composition, boundaries, social institutions, and charismatic roles and functions. This material suggests that mission was an important community task. Chapter 4 establishes a sociology of mission for the community, investigating commitment as the mechanism that motivated community members to pursue mission, the importance of mission to the community, the motivation of converts, and the problems encountered in mission. Chapter 5 investigates the social functions of eschatology in the community and finds that it functioned in legitimating numerous aspects of the community's mission experience. Chapter 6 investigates the social functions of history in the community and finds that it functioned in legitimating various aspects of the community's mission experience.

In the conclusion it is shown that history and eschatology were functionally related to one another in legitimating aspects of the community's mission experience. This functionality also provided a meaningful relationship in helping the community to make sense of its world. This further prepares us to try and understand these ideas theologically by placing them in a social context.

Contexts and meanings: a practical experiment in parable interpretation

Archer, K.M. *Manchester*. PhD. 1991.

This study is a practical experiment in parable interpretation rather than a discussion of hermeneutic theory or an analysis of texts alone (Ch.I). Largely on the basis of Perrin's five-stage interpretation process, a working hermeneutic method is designed for use and test in the chapters that follow. Discussion reveals that assumptions Perrin makes about historical criticism's objectivity are over-optimistic, so his process is simplified into two stages. The first, *reading-out*, should use textual reconstruction, historical criticism and literary criticism to discover the original meaning of 'parables of Jesus'; the second, *reading-in*, should complete interpretation by finding in them meaning for today (Ch.II).

Five parables are selected for the experiment: the Great Supper, the Labourers in the Vineyard, the Two Sons, the Prodigal Son and the Good Samaritan. *Reading-out* begins with the reconstruction of 'parables of Jesus'

(Ch. III). Reflection on this concludes, amongst other things, that even textual reconstruction is an interpretative task (Ch. IV). The parables are read 'performantially' and analysed structurally and the original hearers' understanding of them is reconstructed (Ch. V). The main finding of reflection upon this is that a Gadamerian 'fusion of horizons' has already taken place in *reading-out*. Perrin's concept of interpretation as a linear process ending in 'hermeneutics proper' (his equivalent of *reading-in*) is thus shown to be wrong. *Reading-in* is therefore rethought in the light of Gadamer and a failed experiment in group *reading-in* (Ch. VI), and accordingly modern experience (from the writer's work in Industrial Mission) is juxtaposed against each of these parables (Ch. VII). Reflection on the reader's role throughout the process confirms and expands Gadamer's point that interpretation is a function of tradition, clarifies the difference between its two stages, and enables a new, circular model of it to be drawn. Finally, the value of modern insight from parable interpretation is discussed in the face of Derrida's attack in theology (Ch.VIII). An epilogue pursues this further in broader terms to conclusions which, given the conditions of modern culture, are modestly positive (Ch.IX).

20 Paul's purpose in writing Romans: the upbuilding of a Jewish and Gentile Christian Community in Rome

Lo, L.K. *Durham*. PhD. 1991.

The aim of this thesis is to provide a comprehensive study of Paul's purpose in writing Romans, showing the coherence between the 'frame' and the 'body' of the letter and the relationship between the situation of Roman Christians and the main argument of the letter. In order to bring a more objective approach to the study of the letter, we develop a methodology which we call *personae* analysis. This approach takes Romans seriously as a letter and as Paul's argumentation in the context of the interaction between himself and his addresses.

In Chapter 1, we argue for the feasibility of studying Romans as a letter addressed to the situation in Rome. In Chapter 2 to 4 (Part I), we use information mainly from Roman authors, Jewish authors and the inscriptional data from Roman Jewish catacombs to reconstruct a plausible situation of the Roman Jewish community in the first century C.E. with special reference to social intercourse between Jews and Gentiles.

In Chapter 5 to 8 (Part II), we reconstruct a plausible situation of the Roman Christians and develop a hypothesis of Paul's purpose in writing Romans. We suggest that one of Paul's main purposes in writing the letter is to persuade the Jewish and Gentile Christians in Rome to build up a Christian community network, which he does by arguing in accordance with his understanding of the gospel. With the assumption that Gentile Christians are required to become Jews and Jewish Christians are not expected to relinquish their connection with non-Christian Jews, Paul expects that he can promote the upbuilding of this community net-work by means of his letter before he arrives in Rome to launch his mission to Spain. Thus this community net-work would give concrete support to his mission to Spain and spiritual support for his journey to

Jerusalem. In Chapters 9 to 11 (Part III), we test our hypothesis in a survey of Paul's main argument in the doctrinal core of the letter, Rm. 1-11.

In the conclusion, we draw out from our study some theological, missiological and hermeneutical implications for our understanding of Paul, his letters and his relationship with Judaism.

The relationship between theology and ethics in the letter to the Ephesians

Jeal, R.R. *Sheffield*. PhD. 1990.

The Letter to the Ephesians is comprised of two distinct parts that can be labelled 'theology' (Ephesians 1-3) and 'ethics' (Ephesians 4-6). These sections are, however, difficult to reconcile with each other. The moral exhortations of the paraenesis are not directly and argumentatively derived from the theological narrative.

Although Ephesians is a letter, epistolary analysis does not lead to an explanation of how the 'theological' and 'ethical' sections can be integrated. A rhetorical critical examination, however, provides a new angle of interpretation that shows a way through the difficulties of explaining how the two halves of the letter are related to each other. Ephesians is a document that can be designated as 'sermon'. As a 'sermon' it is a combination of epideictic and deliberative rhetorical genres that does not address a specific issue of controversy. It speaks to a Christian audience that is not expected to make critical decisions based on argumentation within the 'sermon,' but rather is reminded of, impressed with, and identifies with certain theological concepts. A frame of mind is thereby developed among the audience members that make them receptive to the moral exhortations contained in the paraenesis.

An analysis of the 'theological' section of Ephesians reveals that a frame of mind receptive to moral exhortation is developed through the rhetorical presentation of theological notions with which the audience would be in agreement. The 'ethical' section or paraenesis is not directly founded on these theological notions, but presents its own, self-contained argumentation for proper conduct to an audience that has become susceptible to such behavioral appeals.

It is concluded that theology and ethics in Ephesians are related by the rhetorical use of the language of what is defined as 'sermon'.

22 Luke's preface and the synoptic problem

Scott, J.W. *St Andrews*. PhD. 1986.

The preface to Luke's gospel (Lk. 1:1-4), when properly exegeted, says this: "(1) Since many have undertaken to draw up a narrative account of the things that are well-established among us, (2) just as those who from the beginning have been eyewitnesses and servants of the word have handed them down to us, (3) I have decided, for my parts, having been a follower of them all for a long time, to write an accurate narrative for you, most excellent Theophilus, (4) in order that you may know what is certain with regard to the matters in which you have been instructed." Luke's claim to have been a follower of the apostles (v.3), and thus conversant with their oral gospel tradition (v.2), is confirmed by an ecclesiastical tradition that can be traced back to one of those very apostles.

Luke implies that he did not use written sources in the composition of his gospel, for unlike ancient historians who die use written sources, he does not acknowledge any use of his predecessors' narratives. In writing "an accurate narrative" he would not have relied upon what he considered to be the inaccurate narratives of his predecessor. Luke indicates that his gospel records the oral tradition that he has learned directly from the apostles.

The leading theories of synoptic origins tend to collapse into an oral theory under the weight of Luke's literary independence. The arguments hitherto advanced against the oral theory are inadequate. The oral tradition consisted of a basic narrative tradition (which is reconstructed) and a body of independent tradition. Luke and Matthew drew upon both traditions, but Mark confined himself to the former. Our two-tradition theory is corroborated, especially in comparison with the standard two-source theory, by various literary and stylistic phenomena.

23 The Davidic Messiah in Luke-Acts: the promise and its fulfillment in Lukan Christology

Strauss, M.L. *Aberdeen*. PhD.1992.

This work examines one theme within Luke's Old Testament christology, that of the coming king from the line of David. An examination of the first century context of meaning reveals that at the turn of the Christian era there is a widespread and relatively stable hope for a Davidic messiah within a broader context of eschatological diversity. The early Christian communities took up these expectations and applied them to Jesus, confessing him to be the Christ now 'raised up' in fulfillment of scripture. (chs.1-2)

An examination of the birth narrative and the speeches in Acts reveals that Luke shows a strong interest in this Davidic theme, introducing it into passages which are introductory and programmatic for his Christology as a whole. Jesus is the promised messiah, who through his life, death, resurrection, and exaltation-enthronement has fulfilled the promises to David. (chs. 3-4)

Despite this strong royal-messianic presentation in the nativity and in Acts, Luke's programmatic Nazareth sermon portrays Jesus as the *Prophet-herald* of Isaiah 61.1-2. This has caused many scholars to describe Luke's Christology as essentially prophetic, rather than royal. The present work argues that a better solution lies in Luke's reading of Isaiah as a unity, where the eschatological deliverer is at the same time Davidic king (Isa 9, 11), suffering servant of Yahweh (Isa 40-55), and prophet-herald (Isa 61). This synthesis not only fits Luke's Christological portrait and strong interest in Isaiah, but it also explains why Luke presents Jesus' messianic task as an 'exodus' he is about to fulfill in Jerusalem (Lk 9.31). In Isaiah and other prophets, the coming Davidic king is often presented as the agent of the eschatological new exodus (cf. Isa 11.1-16). For Luke Jesus is the Davidic messiah who (like Moses) leads God's people on an eschatological new exodus through suffering as the servant of Yahweh. (chs 5-6)

The artistry of John: the Fourth Gospel as narrative Christology

Stibbe, M. *Nottingham.* PhD. 1989.

The present work has two aims. The first aim is to introduce the method of narrative criticism to New Testament scholars and we attempt to do this in Part One. Narrative criticism of the Bible has been practised since the early 1980's, but since that time no one has established the nature and the aims of the method. This thesis is the first work to define what a comprehensive narrative-critical approach to the gospels might entail. It is also the first work to include historical concerns in the narrative-critical programme. The examples of narrative criticism we do have in New Testament studies all assume that narrative criticism *must* be an a-historical method. We point out the fallacy of this view by drawing attention to the recent sociological studies of the narrative form and to the narrative history debate in History Faculties during the 1960's and 1970's. These two movements in scholarship necessitate a historical dimension to narrative criticism if the narrative form is not to be greatly restricted and oversimplified.

In Part One we provide an apology for narrative criticism and we show how future Johannine scholars might examine JOHN as narrative Christology (chapter one), narrative performance (chapter two), community narrative (chapter three), and narrative history (chapter four). In Part Two we provide an illustration of the method at work. Taking the Johannine passion narrative as our text (John 18-19), we show how this part of JOHN might be examined as narrative Christology (chapter five), narrative performance (chapter six), community narrative (chapter seven) and narrative history (chapter eight). This thesis is the first to expose these chapters to a thorough and rigorous literary approach. Our analysis reveals that the fourth evangelist has constructed his passion story with great artistry. We draw particular attention to narrative echo-effects, characterization, tragic mood, the reader's response of 'home-coming' and time-shapes in John 18-19. These, and many other narrative strategies, contribute towards the classic, disclosing power of JOHN's story of the death of Jesus.

25 The prophetic vision of the Son of Man in the Fourth Gospel

Roffe, T.J. *Newcastle Upon Tyne*. Phd. 1985.

The thesis is a typological study of the Fourth Gospel in the light of its Son of man sayings, paying particular attention to their context within the Gospel; with the four canonical Gospels; and within the Judeo-Christian tradition. It shows the importance for the Fourth Gospel of an aspect within apocalyptic Judaism concerning the vision of the open heaven. The Johannine Son of man theme reflects disputes within Judaism surrounding the vision of God. The Fourth Evangelist reinterprets the Synoptic Son of man tradition, using Old Testament texts central to these disputes, to Jesus the vision of God. Our Evangelist engages in the one hand in an internal dispute with other Christians and on the other hand in an external dispute with Jews. He retells the gospel story, of his own situation. Through his Gospel we see the relation between the Johannine church and the synagogue.

My first three chapters show how the

Evangelist links his Son of man theme to Old Testament vision texts to interpret Jesus as the prophetic vision of the heavenly Son of man (Jn 1:51; 3:13, 14; 5:27). The remaining chapters show how this interpretation affects the community's worship and its relation with the synagogue.

The Fourth Gospel is so different from the Synoptic Gospels. The Son of man theme is common to all four Gospels, and to apocalyptic Judaism. Therefore the conclusions drawn from a reading of the Fourth Gospel can be tested by a comparison with the Synoptic tradition and with the Jewish apocalyptic tradition.

26 The example and teaching of Jesus in Romans 12:1-15:13

Thompson, M.B. *Cambridge*. PhD. 1988.

The primary aim of this thesis is to examine Rom 12:1-15:13 in detail in order to determine whether and how Paul alludes to Jesus tradition (JT).

After an introduction addressing the need, aims, limitations, assumptions, and problems of method, Part One ('Allusions and Illusions') sets the stage for the study of Romans. A chapter on the meaning and detection of allusions defines terms and offers eleven criteria for evaluation parallels. The second chapter summarizes an extensive investigation of JT in the non-Pauline epistles and in the Apostolic Fathers, in order to place Paul in his proper context and to establish realistic expectations. Chapter three completes the prolegomena with a brief discussion of Paul's knowledge and probable attitude toward JT, followed by a collection of factors often cited to explain his lack of explicit reference to Jesus. The hypothesis that Paul would have been positively disposed toward JT is then explored and tested in the remainer of the thesis.

Part Two constitutes the bulk of the dissertation, featuring serial studies of Romans 12:1-15:13 and focusing particularly on verses often claimed to be dominical 'allusions'. Only one verse is a probable allusion (14:14), but many more or less probable echoes appear in the section, indicating the importance of dominical *teaching* for Paul. Other relevant parallel passages (Gal 5-6, 1 Cor 10-11, Phil 2, Col 3) are discussed in the course of investigating the *example* of Christ, which includes reference to the earthly Jesus and which underlies 12:1f; 13.14; and 15:1 before surfacing clearly in 15:3-8. In cases of potential conflict, Jesus' example (seen especially on the cross) takes precedence over his specific teachings for Paul. The dissertation concludes with a summary and ten theses.

27 Monotheism and Christology in 1 Corinthians 8:4-6

Rainbow, P.A. *Oxford. D. Phil. 1987.*

The thesis is a description of the relationship between the 'one God, the Father' and the 'one Lord, Jesus Christ' in 1 Cor. 8.4-6. It analyses Paul's language about God and Christ against the background of contemporary Jewish language about the one God, making use of methodic concepts gleaned eclectically from the structural movement in linguistics and the social sciences. Accordingly, the study falls into two parts: a determination of Paul's Jewish monotheistic presuppositions, and an analysis of 1 Cor. 8.4-6 itself.

Part One uses the Greek Old Testament, the Apocrypha, the Pseudepigrapha, the Dead Sea Scrolls, Philo, Josephus, and the New Testament, in particular some two hundred statements of monotheism collected from these sources (presented in an appendix), to illumine the oblique references to monotheistic belief in Paul's letters. This part of the study concentrates on answering a series of nine questions about Jewish monotheism designed to shed light on Paul's language in our chosen passage. Part Two combines the familiar grammatical-historical methods of biblical scholarship with newer, structural methods of exegesis to investigate the doctrinal content of the quasi-confessional language about God and Christ in 1 Cor. 8.4-6 in the light of our results from Part One.

The major conclusions of the study can be summarized in three statements. (1) 1 Cor. 8.6 contains two classic statements of monotheism using traditional Jewish language, one in reference to the Father and one in reference to Jesus Christ; in each case, the language of monotheism comprehends not only the explicit confession with 'one', but also the prepositional phrases, which contain elements closely associated with belief in one God in Jewish thought. (2) Paul's paradoxical language about

God and Christ in this passage certainly expresses the functional subordination of Christ to God, but it very probably presupposes an identity of these two figures at some undefined point, an identity which may well be essential in nature (by comparison especially with Gal. 4.8). (3) The language about Christ in 1 Cor. 8.6 is informed not so much by Jewish Wisdom speculation as by Jewish language about the one God: it is best labelled a 'monotheism Christology'.

Hence the contribution of the thesis to knowledge lies in three areas. (1) It clarifies the nature and associations of Jewish monotheistic language. (2) It provides scientific support, using the most current methods of exegesis and working with a wide selection of comparative Jewish materials, for the view, by no means generally accepted, that the New Testament adumbrates the concept of the ontological deity of Christ. (3) It brings to the fore a Christological category - the language of monotheism - which has been largely overlooked by researchers in the field of the origins and development of Christology in the early church.

28 The cross in Corinth: functions of Paul's references to the death of Jesus with regard to social world

Pickett, Jr., R.W. *Sheffield*. Ph.D. 1991.

This study of Paul's references to the death of Jesus in the Corinthian correspondence attempts to ascertain what Paul was trying to accomplish in the community by invoking the symbol of the crucified Christ. It is a contextual reading of these two extant letters which analyses the function or social impact this symbol was designed to have in the realm of social interaction. From the letters it can be inferred that the community consists of people from a wide range of socio-economic backgrounds and that the liberating effects of Paul's gospel were the manifest in a variety of ways. These different expressions of freedom were the main cause of the disunity and interpersonal conflict which seem to be Paul's primary concern. Moreover, it is evident from criticisms of Paul reflected in the letters and Paul's descriptions of the attitudes and behaviour of certain Corinthians that the gospel was conceived of in terms of Greco-Roman cultural values associated with social power.

Paul addresses the disunity and conflict which has resulted from self-indulgent abuses of freedom by extending the meaning of the death of Jesus, the symbol upon which this freedom was predicated. The references to the death of Jesus in these letters have both a negative and positive function. Paul emphasizes the weakness and foolishness of the cross to critique the cultural values of power and wisdom which are the basis of claims to superiority in the community. More constructively, Paul invokes the symbol of Christ's death to define the true character of freedom vis-à-vis other members of the community. The death of Christ is death for others, and hence it symbolizes the other-regarding behaviour essential to realizing the vision of community which Paul infers from his gospel and sets before the Corinthians.

29 Obeying the truth: a study of Paul's exhortation in Galatians 5-6

Barclay, J.M.G. *Cambridge.* PhD. 1986.

The aim of the thesis is to analyse Paul's exhortation in Galatians 5-6 in order to gain a clearer understanding of its purpose and its place in the letter. This passage has received a number of different interpretations which are critically reviewed in an introductory chapter. Attention is then focused on the Galatians crisis, especially its two central features: the opponents' demand for circumcision and the Galatians' willingness to observe the law. These suggest that the crisis concerns both the question of membership in the Abrahamic covenant and the question of subsequent covenant obedience. Paul's response to the crisis can be seen to handle both these questions; and an analysis of his arguments in 2:15-5:6 shows his distinctive approach to the Abrahamic covenant and his concern for concentrated in 5:13-6:10, is not unrelated appendix but a necessary part of his description of true covenant obedience.

The exhortation can best be explained as an attempt to assure the Galatians that, if they walk in the Spirit, they will truly fulfill the will of God (5:13-24;6:2), followed by an explanation of how the qualities listed as the fruit of the Spirit can be applied to help settle their present community strife (5:25-6:10). Paul's arguments are aided by the positive nuances in such terms as 'fruit' and the ambiguities inherent in such phrases as 'fulfilling the law'. Moreover, since the term 'flesh' can describe existence under the law (as in 3:3), it appears that the Spirit-flesh dualism is exploited in 5:13-6:10 to include an ironical polemic against submission to the law, which is ranged alongside selfish and libertine behaviour.

This analysis leads to the conclusion that Paul's exhortation served a number of different defensive and argumentative purposes and is an integral part of the letter which complements the earlier arguments. It also allows a number of general observations to be made concerning Pauline ethics and Paul's attitude to the law.

Paul's language about God

Richardson, N.G. *Brunel*. PhD. 1993.

In view of the neglect by scholars until very recently of the New Testament language about God, this study examines the language which Paul uses about God.

First, four passages, varying in context and content, are chosen for detailed examination. From Romans 9-11 the conclusion is drawn that Paul's language and arguments are more radically theocentric than those in comparable passages in contemporary Jewish writings. and that Paul's eschatological and christological perspective has drawn his language about God into new patterns. The same theocentric emphasis can be seen in 1 Corinthians 1:18-3:23, where the words *theos* and *stauros* exercise a sharply critical function in the face of Corinthian pretensions. 2 Corinthians 2:14-4:6 shows a polemical use both of 'God' and 'Spirit', as Paul defends his ministry. This polemical use of the word *Pneuma* is its normal and primary function in Paul's writings. The fourth passage,

Romans 12:1-15:13, shows the same theocentric emphasis, but, at the same time, (as in the early passages), a far-reaching interaction and interdependence between Paul's language about God and his language about Christ.

Two chapters are devoted to an examination of language about God and used by contemporary, or near contemporary Jewish writers, The evidence confirms the findings of earlier chapters that for Paul's the 'centre of gravity' of his language about God has changed. The particularist, apologetic and theodical concerns of Judaism are entirely, or almost entirely, absent from his writings. The comparison suggests that, while there is undoubted continuity between Paul and his Jewish contemporary in their language about God, there are also far-reaching differences.

The use of the Old Testament in the composition of First Peter

Schutter, W.L. *Cambridge.* PhD. 1985.

The current awakening of scholarly interest in 1 Peter has left a problem central to its interpretation largely untouched, the use of Scripture. Already the victim of acute neglect in the modern period, the state of the question is thus falling even further behind relative to where it is in most other New Testament writings. The dissertation seeks to remedy the situation somewhat by clarifying the main hermeneutical presuppositions, methods, and techniques demonstrated by the author of 1 Peter in its composition.

The dissertation has four chapters. The first locates the question in the context of Petrine studies. The second treats certain basic questions as a preliminary to comprehensive literary analysis. The third undertakes a detailed literary-critical examination of the sources the author used, and, by concentrating upon the way they have been integrated, makes it possible to distinguish his handling of Scripture in terms of specific conventions and practices attested for contemporary Judaism and the early Church.

Several major conclusions are reached: 1) 1 Pet. 1:14-2:9 approximates to an early form of homiletic Midrash, 2) 1 Pet, 1:10-2 is the key to the author's hermeneutic, and, 3) many of the uses of Scripture in the letter have formal affinities with applications characteristic of the Qumran community and various New Testament authors.

The relationship between worship and suffering in 1 Peter and Revelation

Holdsworth, J.I. *Cardiff*. PhD. 1992.

1 Peter contains many references to suffering but the nature of the suffering is an open question. Likewise 1 Peter alludes to worship although in exactly what way is not agreed. Revelation is also said to be prompted by experiences of suffering and to witness, perhaps more than any other New Testament Book, to worship; but again, the precise nature of each is uncertain and the relationship between them largely unexplored. Since both books were addressed to approximately the same geographical area within a short time of each other, further study of the various relationships is merited.

The thesis is concerned with the self-understanding of the Christian communities addressed in the books, and seeks to determine what that understanding is by examining the possible range of meanings of 'suffering' in 1 Peter and Revelation. The relationship between this understanding and 'worship' is explored. A critical examination of recent European scholarship provides a working definition of the terms of reference. There follows an extensive analysis of examples in both books.

The thesis finds strong evidence to connect the eucharist and suffering, baptism and suffering, and praise in a more general sense, and suffering. This is true *per se* and is attested, particularly in the books. The questions of the social function of worship in the situation described are addressed under the headings: worship and polemic/apologetic; worship and solidarity/unity; worship as statement of identity; worship as a vehicle of consolation. Some evidence is found for each, but with different emphases. The thesis raises the question as to whether suffering in some substantial evidence for an affirmative conclusion.

The genre of the Book of Revelation from a source-critical perspective

Mazzaferri, F.D. *Aberdeen.* PhD. 1986.

This is a small contribution to the current debate regarding the genre of the Book of Revelation. The study is motivated by the observation that John employs prolific sources both uniquely and generically. The results of prior source critical studies are employed to delineate the scope and nature of John's sources. The specific source-critical contribution of this study is a detailed analysis of the manner in which John employs his sources with generic intent. However, the analysis is conducted in strict compliance with the dictates of the principles of generic criticism.

For convenience, these principles and those of souse criticism are not discussed until just prior to the generic analysis of Revelation itself. But the initial chapters assume the principles to lay the necessary groundwork. A study of authorship and unity indicates that Rev is a unified whole, the work of a single author. Source criticism may therefore be confined alone to John's prolific allusions and punctilious quotations. Generic definitions are deduced for classical OT prophecy and classical apocalyptic in turn. However, available data is far too sparse to permit similar results for NT prophecy or neo-apocalyptic. Accordingly, only the first two have any possible generic claim upon Revelation.

In strict generic terms Revelation fails to qualify as classical apocalyptic, as indicated as well by source criticism. Generically, Revelation also fails to qualify as classical prophecy. However, generic and source criticism concur that John makes strenuous efforts to match this paradigm, and falls only marginally short. He is certainly a neo-classical prophet, albeit with no generic companions. He dips his hand in several diverse families of sources. But he bathes himself in classical OT prophecy alone.

Friendship: a way of interpreting Christian love
Carmichael, E.D.H. *Oxford*. D.Phil. 1990.

How is Christian love to be understood? Is it a one-way love: a desire that rises towards God, or a perfectly selfless altruism? Does it include or deny, love of self? The thesis presented is that love is relationship and the central case of relationship is friendship. It is demonstrated that there exists a body of thought, within the Western Christian tradition, which has interpreted Christian love in terms of friendship, and outgoing Christian love as an offer of friendship.

Chapter One presents the classical tradition of friendship, from Homer to Rome, with special reference to Aristotle's *Nicomachean Ethics* VIII-IX and Cicero's *De Amicitia*. Chapter Two considers problems, including biblical and patristic usage, and establishes the legitimacy of using the language of friendship in theology; it introduces positive arguments for the interpretation of Christian love as friendship.

This interpretation is studied in the *De Officiis Ministrorum* of Ambrose, Aelred's *Speculum Caritatis* and *De Spiritali Amuicitia*, in several works of Thomas Aquinas including the *Summa Theologiae*, in the *Discourse of Friendship* by Jeremy Taylor, and in explorations of Christ as 'friend' and 'open friendship' by Jurgen Moltmann. Each of these five Chapters is extrapolated to indicate further developments.

This study presents both the practice of Christian love as friendship, and its theological roots and implications; it concludes that the love revealed by Christ should be understood in terms of friendship, actual or potential. Relationship is intrinsic to the divine nature, and the love of Christ on the cross is that of a friend who wills to draw all into friendship. Christian love as friendship is grounded on shared nature or grace; it expresses itself in action; it respects the other and is present to them, desiring, without demanding, the joy of reciprocity.

35 Tertullian's understanding of death and the afterlife

Imarie, J.M. *Edinburgh*. PhD. 1992.

'The blood of the Christians is the seed'. This aphorism regarding the 'seed' of the Church is probably Tertullian's most memorable assertion regarding death. However, it would be misleading, indeed dangerously simplistic to confine his reflections on death to the theme of 'bearing witness'.

The thesis seeks to demonstrate the complexity of Tertullian's reflections on death. Taking as its point of departure the physical phenomenon itself, the thesis explores, in turn, the six most prominent themes within the Tertullianic understanding of death. The said themes are death as a physical phenomenon, death as the imitation of Christ, death as a teaching medium, death as the culmination of man's conflict with the powers of evil, death as the ultimate sacrifice and death as the gateway to the hereafter.

Did Tertullian regard death as 'natural'? Did he formulate a 'scientific' theory of death and putrefaction? Can a vision of discipleship which primarily focuses upon the motifs of 'indebtedness' and 'enslavement' be characterized as a genuine expression of 'imitatio Christi'? Did Tertullian regard the shedding of blood as a symbol of 'life' given over to death or did he simply regard it as a symbol of 'death' and 'violence'? Was his concept of martyrdom modified by his memories of the sacrificial demands of the Romano-Punic deities, Ba'al Hammon/Saturn and Tanit/Caelestics? These are but a few of the questions addressed by the thesis.

36 Creation theology in Origen

Haers, J.R.M. *Oxford*. D.Phil. 1992.

Two major claims are made in this thesis. (1) Origen uses the concept of creation primarily to refer to the relationship between the Creator and his rational creatures. Seen from this perspective, the idea of creation acquires existential significance for Origen's hearers and readers. (2) Creation is a central concept in Origen's theology not only in the sense that it represents a junction at which various important themes of his thought meet (Trinity, cosmology, anthropology, Christology, eschatology,...), but also because it is profoundly connected to the form of Origen's theology, which can be characterized as spiritual and Scriptural.

Part I of this thesis represents an analysis of Origen's practice of theology, taking advantage of the results of recent research in Origen: the importance of Origen's homilies over against that of his more dogmatic works, the existential feature of his use of the allegorical method, and the difficulty to classify him as belonging to any one of the currents of thought that dominated the period in which he lives, are particularly emphasized.

Part II deals with Origen's exegesis of the first chapters of *Genesis*, especially in his first homily in *Genesis*. In this homily the relational and existential features of Origen's understanding of the concept of creation appear in the form of two related tensions: that of allegory and that of the dynamics involved in the idea of double creation.

Once the dynamics of Origen's understanding of creation have been clarified, more detailed analyses of specific elements of his approach can be worked out by referring to the more systematic parts of his manoeuvre. Part III does so in the case of some of the protological dimensions of the concept of creation. This analysis leads to a deeper understanding of Origen's ideas on dualism and on the human person.

Prayer and miracle in the spirituality of St. Augustine

Jackson, M.G.St. A. *Cambridge*. PhD. 1986.

This thesis examines, primarily from the standpoint of the original writings, the role envisaged by Augustine of Hippo for prayer and miracle in the spiritual life of the Christian. Understanding both as in accordance with the continuing providential activity of God subsequent to the initial creation, he uses the theory of signs to explain their position in the gradual re-formation of the spiritual sensibilities of fallen man in the material world. Into a broadly Neo-platonic understanding of the relationship between material and spiritual world Augustine injects the idea of re-interpretation of the material as vehicle to the spiritual rather than its automatic ejection as a hindrance. The material can, thus, assist man, while he underlines a gradual process of correction of spiritual response, to re-focus in God at work in and through the material.

Chapter Two and Three examine how miracle

and answered prayer are understood by Augustine to run in parallel in relation to this process of spiritual re-orientation. Miracle is seen as God's adaptation of the customary course of nature and having as its purpose the eliciting of a particular spiritual purpose. Answered prayer is, likewise, God's response to a correct spiritual attitude whereas an incorrect attitude occasions either delay or refusal. Chapter Four sets the question of correct and incorrect spiritual attitude on the part of men in a wider context, tracing a continuity between the attitudes of men and of angels, so that good men approximate to the aspirations of good angels in seeking the blessed life while on earth, and evil men stand in a parallel continuity with evil angels in seeking satisfaction in the lower and material. Chapter Five examines in greater detail the role particularly of prayer in the conforming of the human to the divine will, tracing a broad continuity of attitude by Augustine to the problem of the relationship between human and divine wills from his early writings through to his last. In Chapter Six are drawn together, with reference to discussions in previous chapters, the ways in which the life and work of Christ on earth are pivotal in Augustine's understanding of the correct response of the Christian in the *peregrinatio* to prayer and miracle.

38
St. Augustine of Hippo on Christ, his Church, and the Holy Spirit: a study of the De baptismo and the Tractates in Iohannis evangelium

Clancy, F.G. *Oxford.* D.Phil. 1992.

This study investigates the synthesis between the Christological and Pneumatological dimensions of the Church in Augustine's *De Baptisimo* and the *Tractates on John*. This particular approach was suggested by the stress placed by Zizioulas and Congar on the need to balance these two dimensions in formulating an adequate ecclesiology, and Augustine's own statement relating Trinity and Church in *Enchiridion* 56

Part I is devoted to the *De Baptisimo*, one of Augustine's main anti-Donatist works which simultaneously facilitates some comparisons with Cyprian. Part 2 investigates the *Tractates* on *John* which span a 14-year period of Augustine's preaching. The concluding chapter includes some summary comparisons with Augustine's *De civitate Dei*. A 3-fold objective characterizes the approach to each text: (a) a description of the range of ecclesial images used, their background, and inter-relationship; (b) an analysis of the relationship between Christ and the Church; (c) a parallel examination of the Pneumatological dimension of the Church. The methodology adopted sought to respect the genre, historical context, and integral nature of the texts studied.

This study indicates Augustine's preference for a mosaic of inter-related images, mutually illuminating each other. An ecclesial Christology emerges revealing Christ's intimate association with the different images. The *Tractates* regularly relate the details of Christ's life to the Church. Christ's involvement in the Church's ministry is particularly stressed in both texts. The Pneumatological dimension of the Church is expressed primarily in terms of the preservation of ecclesial unity and the life of charity between her members. Augustine specifically associates Christ and the Spirit in tandem with reference to many features of the *ecclesia*.

The findings of this thesis suggest the need for a corrective to Zizioulas' under-evaluation of the Western ecclesiological tradition in general, and Augustine's pneumatology in particular, especially with reference to emphasis on communion and eschatology.

The knowledge and consciousness of Christ in the light of the writings of St. John of the Cross

Ocd, I.M. *Oxford*. D.Phil. 1991.

In Part A the thesis reviews treatments of Jesus' awareness in contemporary exegesis, and in the theological elaborations of Aquinas and of Rahner, Lonergan and Galot. The limitations they encounter - paucity of evidence, artificially, the difficulty of finding a credible model for a unique Jesus - invite us to consider the testimony of the mystics. We turn to Juan (John of the Cross), not for evidence of how Jesus' hypostasis related to consciousness, but for testimony to the possibilities of human experience of the divine, which might then help our understanding of Jesus' human experience of his Father.

Part B examines Juan's treatment of union with God. We first establish criteria for recognizing where Juan's account is based on his experience. We propose the *Living Flame* as his most experimental commentary, and consider its hermeneutic. We draw from it the characteristics of the bride-soul who has reached union, relate those to Juan's wider theological system, and to the possibilities of awareness and expression. We attempt to apply the resulting picture to the case of Jesus, and find it a helpful contextualisation of what exegetes and theologians had proposed. Still, the application is tentative, especially where Juan's treatment of night and faith is concerned.

Part C therefore considers how Juan himself understood his experience to relate to Jesus - beginning with the 'Romances' where experience and Christology touch most nearly. In their light we examine the nuptial Christology of Juan's major works, and find Juan affirming that his experience derives from and depends on that of the earthly Jesus now risen. In both the exalted union of the *Living Flame* and the extreme suffering of *Night*, Jesus is Juan's form. On these terms we should not ignore Juan's testimony to union and suffering in considering what it meant to be Jesus.

40 Social and political aspects of the career of St. Basil of Caesarea

Beagon, P.M. *Oxford*. D.Phil. 1990.

This thesis attempts to bring an amalgam of approaches, theological and historical, to the life and work of St. Basil of Caesarea, to illuminate the social and political history of Cappadocia in the second half of the fourth century AD. The work is divided into four chapters. Chapter One attempts to evoke the physical environment of late antique Cappadocia. It is argued that a proper geographical understanding is necessary to appreciate fully Basil' s social and political activity. This is particularly the case because the standard accounts of the political geography of Cappadocia are erroneous in several respects. It is argued that the correct location of a number of key towns casts new light in the motives for Basil' s episcopal activity. The focus in Chapter Two narrows to concentrate on the relationship between Basil and his congregation. This is done by a close study of the martyr-sermons attributed to Basil. This study is placed in the wider context of the growth in the martyrs-curt at this time.

The way in which Basil used the martyrs in the problems he faced as bishop is highlighted. Links are made with Chapter One by a consideration of the evidence for *martyria* in the environs of Caesarea. Chapter Three concentrates on Basil's relationship with the emperor Valens. This is shown to be more complex and less antagonistic than the traditional accounts in the ecclesiastical histories would have one believe. Finally, Chapter Four attempts to provide a sketch of the 'cultural geography' of Basil's life by using a selected sample of his letters. It argues against the crude use of the concepts 'Christian' and 'Pagan' in seeking to explain Basil's activity. Particular attention is paid to the alleged correspondence between Basil and Libanius, some of which at least, it is argued, is genuine.

41 The Desert Fathers on personal relationships

Gould, G.E. *Cambridge*. PhD. 1989.

The *Apophthegmata Patrum* is a large collection of sayings and stories about the fourth and fifth century Egyptian monks known as the Desert Fathers. The text of the *Apophthegmata* may be seen as a witness to a monastic community which was concerned to maintain its own coherence and identity, and as the ultimate product of a relatively reliable and disciplined oral tradition. The primary locus of this tradition was the encounter between the Abba (or spiritual father) and his disciple. The *Apophthegmata* show a far-reaching concern with the nature of this relationship, which the Desert Fathers saw as a personal relationship (rather than one based on the impersonal exercise of authority) involving, on the part of disciple, obedience and surrender of his own will, and on the part of Abba, a commitment to teach by example rather than precept. The Desert Fathers' concern extends from the teaching relationship to relationships in general. The cultivation of good relations with his neighbour was an essential part of a monk's formation in the monastic life, and the quality of his relationship with God was directly dependent on his attitudes towards his neighbour. The Desert Fathers show a particular awareness of the problems caused by anger, slander and judgment, and their teaching on personal relationships is dominated by a strong desire to avoid and overcome these unwanted responses and attitudes to others. Their teaching on the communal meal or agape of the monastic community and on hospitality, although dominated by the problem of whether it was right to break a personal fast in order to eat with others, also illustrates their awareness of the importance of good relationships. Many sayings consider the value of solitude in the monastic life, or discuss the reasons for which it is right for a monk to flee from others or change his dwelling-place. These too illuminate the Desert Fathers' understanding of personal relationships. Although a life of prayer and *hesychia* might sometimes be seen as an alternative to a life of engagement with others, the Desert Fathers did try on occasions to explore the corporate significance of prayer and ecstatic or visionary experience.

Christology and anthropology in the spirituality of Maximus the confessor

Madden, J.N. *Durham*. Ph.D. 1983.

The purpose of this thesis is to throw into relief the principal ideas about Christology and Anthropology in the thought of St. Maximus the Confessor. This has been undertaken from the point of view of spirituality, which may be described as theology lived. I have chosen the *Expositio Orationis Dominicae* as the basis of this study because it is one of the most synthetic of Maximus' writings and I believe that an examination of its implications is a way into his theology as a whole. In Chapter 1, I have presented the evidence for his life as an attempt to answer the question: "Who is Maximus?" We find that the personal character of his thought reflects his Christian identity so that his spirituality was indeed theology lived. Chapter 2 is an investigation of the way in which he did theology and provides as well a short account of his works and their contents. Again it becomes obvious that his theology was the fruit of his way of life, both because of the way he understood it as a science and because of the subjects that engaged his attention. In Chapter 3, I examine the *Expositio Orationis Dominicae* in order to grasp something of its linguistic and structural quality. This affords an opportunity of observing Maximus in profile, so to speak, and complements Chapter 2 because of the unconscious way in which he reveals the spiritual nature of his approach to the task of doing theology. Chapter 4 is the principal part of the thesis. It examines the five areas of theological interest that emerge in the *Expositio*: theology and sonship by grace; equality of honour with the angels; participation in divine life; restoration of nature to itself; purification from the law of sin and the abolition of the tyranny of the Evil One. The Prologue and Introductions to the Expositio provide an opportunity of prefacing the main commentary with Maximian insights into agape and the place of mediation in the divine plan. Chapters 5 and 6 treat of the Christological and Anthropological dimensions respectively. The

Expositio is constructed on the basis of the notions of *kenois* and *theosis*, which on scrutiny are seen to be parallel to theology and life. Therefore spirituality will be theology lived in such a way that *kenois* will issue in *theosis* through *agape* exercised in virtue and prayer.

43 Knowledge, faith and philosophy in Thomas Aquinas

Jenkins, J.I. *Oxford*. D.Phil. 1989.

Chapter 1 attempts to elucidate Aquinas's view on the nature of natural knowledge by examining his account of our knowledge of natural kinds. Assuming that in addition to true belief a further condition or conditions are necessary for knowledge, I say an agent who has realized the further condition or conditions is *epistemically justified*. I then ask: what, according to Aquinas, is a subject's epistemic justification for the belief that his putative natural kind ideas are genuine? After arguing against B. Lonerkan's influential interpretation, I present my own view that Aquinas was an externalist about involved factors to which the epistemic subject does not have privileged access (e.g. the subject's cognitive faculties were well designed and are operating properly). According to this epistemological externalism, questions of epistemic rationality are to be distinguished from those of epistemic justification, and I go on to put forward a general account of epistemic rationality. I conclude the chapter with rebuttals to a series of objections, and in the first of these I argue for the consequential claim that Aquinas held an externalism for concepts, which is the view that the individuation of a subject's concepts depends upon the subject's environment.

The next two chapters (II & III) prepare for the chapter on faith (IV). Chapter II summarizes Aquinas's views on nature, natural potencies and the natural and supernatural goods. Special attention is given to the relationship between descriptive claims about human nature and normative claims of the natural law, and I try to bring greater clarity to this matter by applying the results of the investigation of chapter I. Chapter III reviews Aquinas's account of grace and the theological virtues. I consider, firstly, the universal natural order and God's actions within it, secondly, obedient potency and, thirdly, grace and the theological virtues.

Chapter IV examines the epistemic justification and rationality of the assent of faith. After arguing against a widely held naturalist interpretation of the epistemic justification of faith, and against J. Ross's voluntarist interpretation, I present my own supernatural externalism interpretation. It is (epistemologically) *externalis*, for among the conditions of the positive epistemic status of faith is that the subject has certain cognitive faculties properly designed to arrive at the truth in relevant matters. (i.e. of divine revelation), and that the assent is produced by such faculties when operating properly. It is *supernatural* insofar as it understands the faculties in question as the result of a gift or grace God bestows over and above the faculties one has by merely human nature. I then consider the voluntary character and epistemic rationality of faith. Chapter V concludes that, given the results of chapter IV, it is likely that Aquinas's philosophical views were influenced by revealed theology and that it would have been rational for Aquinas to have allowed such an influence.

44 Incarnation and inspiration: John Owen and the coherence of Christology

Spence, A.J. London, *King's College*. PhD. 1989.

Incarnation and inspiration are concepts which can be used to characterize two difference ways of thinking about Christ. Although the history of doctrine suggests they are mutually exclusive, the argument of this thesis is that John Owen successfully integrated them into one coherent Christology.

The underlying structure of his exposition was that of the incarnation, understood as the Son's act of condescension whereby he willingly assumed human nature into personal subsistence with himself. This assumed humanity maintained its integrity in all its operations experiencing God always as man. To the question 'How did the divine Son act in his own human nature?' Owen answered that he did so indirectly and by means of the Holy Spirit.

The distinctive work of the Spirit is the

establishment of the Church by the restoration to it of the image of God. The prototype or foundation of this work of renewal was laid in the humanity of Christ, which the spirit formed, sanctified, empowered, comforted and glorified. Owen thus affirmed an inspirational Christology within the framework of an Alexandrian interpretation of the incarnation.

The coherence of this account is tested with respect to four areas of concern. Firstly, can a Christology which affirms the distinct operation of Christ's two natures successfully maintain the unity of his personal action? Secondly, is nature or ontological language too static to model the dynamic reality of Christ? Thirdly, is Owen justified in arguing that, other than in its assumption, the divine Son acts on his own human nature only indirectly and by means of the Spirit? Fourthly, does Owen's interpretation of the distinct action of the Trinitarian persons undermine the doctrine of the indivisibility of their external operations?

Faith in the theology of Dietrich Bonhoeffer
Sifobela, L.M.M. *London, King's College.* PhD. 1992.

This thesis understands Bonhoeffer as discussing the subject of faith from a Lutheran theological background. It takes the theology of the concreteness in Bonhoeffer as another Luther's version of presenting the issue of 'the good work of faith'. It is on this basis that I have suggested that there is a reappraisal on Luther's theology in Bonhoeffer. It suggests that Bonhoeffer has rendered Luther's theology the service of 'a right hand man' and sees Bonhoeffer to be loyal to the Lutheran theological heritage.

The thesis accords Bonhoeffer the status of a theologian who has been loyal to the traditional Christian doctrines. He is understood as making effort in applying concretely traditional doctrines in space and time, and demanding from the visible church theology and theologian's concrete affirmation of the faith. The thesis sees the subject of faith as central in the theology of

Bonhoeffer and suggests a hypothesis that faith is educator for Living. From this perspective of my exposition on Bonhoeffer (which is the thesis) I think that the presence of faith in believers is the cause and basis on which society is analysed by Christians. When Christians re-examine their life and life situations, they are taught by faith to live in the world. It means that Christian decision is the decision and action of faith. This is the central thrust of the thesis.

The thesis sees Bonhoeffer as presenting great challenges for the doctrinal and traditional claims of the visible church to which Bonhoeffer offers no challenge but a form of loyalty. There is, therefore, a 'mobile' tendency in the self presentation of Bonhoeffer in his theological thoughts. Nevertheless, the thesis accords him the status of the theologian with human touch, feeling and concern and, therefore, suggests that theology is the 'watch dog' for the human community.

The relationship between revelation and religion in the theology of Karl Barth and his critics

Burton, B.D. *Queen's University*. Belfast. PhD. 1991.

One of the most significant yet greatly neglected and often misinterpreted aspects of Karl Barth's theology is his Christian theology of religion(s) based upon his understanding of the relationship between revelation and religion. Karl Barth has made a positive contribution to the development of a Christian theology of religion in the twentieth century, indicated by his continuing influence among contemporary theologians, critics and followers alike.

A proper interpretation of Barth's theology of religion will recognize the primary theological principles/concepts which he utilizes. They are: (1) his affirmation of the centrality of the self-revelation of God in Jesus Christ in relation to all human knowledge and experience of God; (2) his utilization of the dialectical concept of the Aufhebung to describe the relationship between divine revelation and all human religion, while on the other hand revelation may exalt human religion to become "true religion" and to be utilized by God as a parable of the kingdom, bearing witness to the one light, one Word and one Truth of God in Jesus Christ; (3) his doctrines of election and reconciliation and redemption within which the christological balance between exclusiveness (i.e. Jesus Christ is the only means of humanity's election, reconciliation and redemption) and inclusiveness (i.e. in Jesus Christ all humanity is elected , reconciled and possibly redeemed) is maintained.

I believe that Barth provides Christian theology with a comprehensive paradigm for understanding the relationship between Christian revelation and all human religion, namely, the paradigm of exclusive-inclusivism, thereby transcending the traditional polarity between exclusivism and inclusivism without adopting the relativist/pluralist paradigm. This is the promise of Karl Barth's Christian theology of religion(s).

47

Human fallenness: a comparative study in the theologies of Paul Tillich and Karl Rahner

Kidd, R.L. *Oxford*. D.Phil. 1987.

The purpose of this thesis is to examine the concept of human fallenness through a comparative study in the theologies of Paul Tillich and Karl Rahner.

Section One forms an initial inquiry into the theme and its place in the work of these writers. It argues that a contemporary concept of human fallenness, one which does not provoke irreconcilable conflict with what is broadly termed 'scientific' thinking, must be framed in 'existential' terms, a criterion with which Tillich and Rahner seemingly comply.

Section Two analyses Tillich's idea of the fall and Rahner's idea of original sin, and offers a preliminary critique. In Tillich, the question is whether his emphasis on 'ontology' is compatible with his strong affirmation of human freedom; in Rahner, the question is whether his continuing emphasis in the 'historical' origin of sin is compatible with his intention to create a genuinely 'modern' theology.

Section Three, the substance of the thesis, examines four major topics inseparably connected with the concept of humanity as fallen: 'finite freedom', 'the meaning of symbols', 'the historicity of myth' and 'human destiny'. In each the work of comparison is enlisted to provide constructive insights into fallenness as the controlling theme. In this section, a fundamental theological decision about the 'dialectical' relationship between the finite and the infinite emerges as the issues of central importance. It is argued that a credible concept of human fallenness demands not only the use of existential 'categories', but, like Tillich, a commitment to make the dynamic structure of each 'moment' the primary focus for the analysis of reality.

Section Four, a final appraisal, concludes that the theology of Karl Rahner remains too tightly bound to its roots in Aquinas to support an acceptable concept of human fallenness, but that the more thoroughly 'existentialist' theology of Paul Tillich provides significant foundations on which such a concept can be built.

Evangelical theology 1857-1900

Culbertson, E.M. London, *King's College*. PhD. 1991.

This thesis deals with evangelical theology in the Church of England between the years 1857 and 1900. It relates, evaluates and analyses how evangelicals employed their theology in answering controversially rationalist and ritualist theories and new ideas regarding the after-life, and also how evangelicals expressed their theology positively concerning God, creation and evolution, scripture, the last things, the atonement, and the church, sacraments and the liturgy.

In the course of this analysis the present low evaluation of evangelical theologians, especially T.R. Birk and Nathaniel Dimock, is questioned and their reputation enhanced. The assumption that their position was unimaginative and almost uniformly ultra-conservative is shown to be untenable. The lack of scholarly study of these thinkers is remedied.

In an introduction previous scholarship is reviewed, and the importance and relevance of the subject is shown. In chapter one, it is related how evangelicals replied to *Essays and Reviews*, Colenso, Renan, and Seeley and evolutionary thought by relying in a high, though not uniformly verbal theory of Biblical inspiration.

Chapter two deals with rationalism from 1879-1900 and notes a growing breadth in evangelical scholarship. Chapter three concerns the after-life, and shows how some evangelicals accepted that the pains of hell were less severe that traditionally believed.

Chapter four notes the evangelical view of baptismal regeneration, confession, the real presence and eucharistic presence. Chapter five contrasts Garbett and Birks in the 1860s and Moule and Litton in the 1890s on God and creation and describes Birk's impressive assault on evolutionary philosophy.

Chapter six shows how scriptural views varied from the conservative Birks to the liberal Lias. Chapter seven is in the Last Things and the Atonement and chapter eight considers the remarkable liturgical scholarship of Dimock. In the conclusion evangelical theology is contextualised and the implications of its importance considered.

49

The concept of the vicarious humanity of Christ in the theology of Thomas Forsyth Torrance

Kang, P.S. *Aberdeen*. PhD.1983.

This study is an attempt to show that the heart of Thomas Forsyth Torrance's theology is the vicarious humanity of Jesus Christ. It is this vicarious humanity understood in the light of the incarnation of the Word that prescribes to Christian theology "both its matter and its content". Because God in his lordly freedom and mercy has chosen the way of the incarnation, Jesus Christ the incarnate Word is the one and only ontological ground of our being reconciled to God, our knowing of him, and our response to him.

Against the dualist framework of much of modern Christology which tries to distinguish between a Christ of faith and a Jesus of history, Torrance emphasizes a unitary approach which takes together both the theological Jesus and the historical Jesus in order that we may truly understand him out of his own intrinsic significance. This unitary approach is indebted to the

Judaeo-Christian tradition of the Scriptures. Indeed, any understanding of Jesus Christ is bound to be a distortion when severed from the witness of the Jews and of the apostles. Above all, Israel the Jews constitute the pre-history of the incarnation and Christ the Jew their τελος.

Furthermore, the unitary approach implies that we have to take the very-God and very-man Jesus Christ seriously in his one incarnate reality. In this God-man, we have a true Mediator between God and man. Because Jesus is ομοουσιος with the Father, he does not simply communicate something of God but is himself the *self-communication* of God; he is not merely the way to salvation but *is* the Life and the Resurrection. On the other hand, because Jesus Christ is truly man, he assumes our adamic natures into himself, sanctifies and restores it in himself so that we may now be lifted up in the Spirit and participate in his new humanity.

To truly adhere to the vicarious humanity of Jesus Christ as the ontological ground of our faith is to really believe in the sheer Grace of God. Furthermore, this applies not only to our knowledge of God and our redemption in him, but applies as much to our very Christian living and response to God. We can have no faith, no conversion, no worship that is acceptable in the sight of the Father except when our response is graciously gathered up by Christ, the substitutionary and representative Man, in his one and only vicarious response to God.

The concept of regeneration in Christian thought

MacMillan, I.W. *Edinburgh*. PhD. 1986.

Who is the Christian? What does it mean to be a "new man" in Christ? What does it mean to be "born again"? Is this the same as the Pentecostal expression "the baptism in the Holy Spirit"? And what are we to make of the phrase, "the baptism in/with the Holy Spirit"? What is the relationship between water baptism and spirit baptism? What is the relation of regeneration to baptism? Does baptism alone constitute the complete rite of initiation, or is something more required? How is a person's initiation into the Christian way to be described and understood? What is Christian baptism? What is its place in the plan of salvation? When is the Holy Spirit given?

In search of an authentic theology of the Christian, we have treated the writings of the Fourth Evangelist, Cyril of Jerusalem and Ambrose of Milan, John Calvin, Karl Barth and modern day Pentecostalists and Neo-Pentecostalists.

The work, although not divided into specific parts, has two aspects. First of all, there is a full exposition of how the term, "regeneration", has been treated in each of the above theologies. From this it can be seen that various interpretations of the concept have emerged in the church over the centuries.

The second aspect is an examination of four critical categories surrounding our theme, namely, regeneration, initiation, water baptism and spirit baptism. Today is an opportune time to understand the various inter-relationships of these categories, both from the point of view of the pastoral ministry of the churches and the life of the individual Christian.

In the course of our study, various other topics are touched upon: the nature of faith, the relation of baptism to confirmation, the paedobaptist debate, the need to restore a Spirit Christology either alongside, or instead of, Logos Christology, the nature of the gift of speaking in tongues and its place in the fellowship of the church. Each of these subjects requires a thesis of its own, and we have by no means exhausted their significance, although they have necessitated comment because of their relationship to our central theme.

51 The Trinity and the contemporary doctrine of God

Black, A.B.S. *Westminster College*. PhD. 1988.

The Christian understanding of the nature of God is classically expressed in the form of the doctrine of the Trinity. 'The European mind' (Paul Hazard) of the modern period, however, has turned away from this conclusion of the hard pressed debates of Christianity's earliest days. The vicissitudes of religious belief, 'theistic' as much as 'atheistic', have relegated it merely to the status of a post-script (Schleiemacher) - until the coming of Karl Berth's *Church Dogmatics* in 1932! The Barthian legacy has completed contemporary theology to re-evaluate this foundational doctrine. Our first and second chapters therefore rehearse and review some leading contributions to the current debate on the Trinity, beginning with Karl Barth himself. But this whole discussion is presently rather diverse and unfocussed; there is the need to highlight and address some major underlying themes of the debate.

This is one of the purposes of chapter 3. The other is to have clearly before us those issues which any contemporary articulation and/or model of the Trinity has to be able to accommodate. Just so, we examine the three concerns of the interaction of divine and human freedom, God's historicality and the 'pathos' of God. Our fourth and final chapter involves returning to the Scriptural witness to God's primordial revelation in and through Jesus Christ, in order to construct a new model of the trinitarian nature of God, which might serve some of these major needs of today's Western Church, while remaining faithful to certain basic patterns of the Faith. The revised definition of Christian deity, of which the model is its 'summary concept' (Jungel), is then analysed phrase by phrase.

52 The logic and language of the incarnation: towards a Christology of identification

McEnhill, P. St. Andrews. PhD. 1993.

This thesis provides an examination of the contemporary discussion of incarnational language as it receives classical expression in the formulations of the Council of Chalcedon in 451 A.D. with a view to developing an incarnational account based on God's identification with Jesus of Nazareth. With this in view consideration is given to a number of contemporary defenses of the logic of Chalcedon viewed as a literal statement of identity. It is argued that such defenses fail in that they carry over the tensions inherent in Chalcedon unresolved into their own positions. From this conclusion consideration is given to the criticism that incarnational language is not literal but metaphorical. This is agreed, but an argument is offered to show that metaphors can refer and bear cognitive information and as such are capable of conceptual articulation. It is further argued that there is an important class of metaphors which are 'theory-constitutive' such that the theoretical claims which they embody cannot be expressed apart from the metaphor. An attempt is made to show that the metaphor of incarnation is one such 'theory-constitutive' metaphor.

The results of this general discussion of incarnational language are then applied to the chiristological theories of Theodore of Mopsuestia and Donald Baillie. It is argued that they are legitimate and proper attempts to articulate the claims embodied in the metaphor of incarnation. An attempt is made to show that they offer a genuine middle way between Chalcedon and purely inspirational accounts of the incarnation. However, it is conceded that the traditional question raised against these theories, as to whether or not they can successfully maintain a unity of person, is a legitimate one, given their failure to indicate adequately how the union operated.

53 The Holy Spirit and religious experience in Christian literature c.90-200

Morgan-Wynne, J.E. *Durham*. PhD. 1987.

This thesis explores whether religious experience and the Spirit are linked in Christian literature between c.90 and 200. Three spheres of religious experience were chosen as illustrations - a sense of being personally encountered/overwhelmed by the divine; of divine illumination/guidance; and of being divinely empowered for ethical conduct.

The introduction reviews precious research: since Weinel there has not been a comprehensive survey covering both the New Testament and early Patristic evidence, in what is the transition period between the subapostolic church and the emergence of the catholic church by the early third century. A brief survey of the evidence before c.90 sets the background for the study.

Thereafter, the thesis is divided into a further seven parts, surveying the literature on a geographical basis, viz Syria, Asia Minor, Greece, Rome, Southern Gaul, Northern Africa and Egypt.

The final part draws together the conclusions of the study. Whether the Spirit was at different moments a part of Christian distinctiveness over against the world, Judaism and internal opponents, whether deemed 'heretical' or not, is explored.

The evidence for a continuing sense of being overwhelmed by an encounter with the Holy Spirit is patchy, and no uniform type of experience necessarily emerges within any given geographical area. Throughout the period Christians were confronted by the need to test claims to inspiration by the Spirit. None of the various tests proposed really centred on the actual experience itself but all were external ones.

Claims to possess the truth took various forms, and again there was no necessary uniformity with any given area. Generally, the ethical demand and the Spirit's help was less held together than was characteristic of Paul. Some writers may mention both aspects but these were not expressed in a integrated way; others came close to moralism. The variegated picture which emerges probably faithfully reflects second century Christianity.

The Puritan meditative tradition, 1599-1691: a study of ascetical piety

Chan, S.K.H. *Cambridge*. PhD. 1986.

54

The study of the puritan meditative tradition reveals a distinct type of piety which emerged among the godly of the late Elizabethan church. The tradition was based on a mediate conception of grace (ch. 1). It drew on certain aspects of Calvin's thought but it grew directly out of the peculiar devotional instinct of English Protestantism. Among the early English protestants, meditation was not clearly distinguished from prayer (ch. 2), but a theory of and practical approach to meditation began to emerge with Richard Greenham, William Perkins, Richard Rogers and Joseph Hall (ch. 3). In Greenham and Perkins we discover a theory of meditation and some application of it in certain devotional exercises. Richard Rogers took meditation a step further by installing it as a 'set' exercise in his systematic devotional guide, and so, 'technicalised' it. Finally, Hall ensured a more permanent place for mediation in the puritan *regula vitae* by reducing it to a set of cultivable skills.

The coming of age of meditation in Hall was followed by the extensive application of the meditative technique in practically all stages of the ordosalutis, making the cultivation of godliness a process bearing striking similarities with the traditional 'three ways'. The meditative paradigm was applied to the 'purgative' processes of 'preparation' as well as the regulation of thought and affections (ch. 4); to certain private and public religious exercises observed on a regular basis which correspond roughly to the illuminative way (ch. 5); and to heavenly meditation, from which a distinct contemplative strain emerged. Chronologically and logically, the tradition could well be said to culminate in Richard Baxter who saw in heavenly meditation the consummation of the Christian's spiritual experience on earth (ch. 6). The result of the cultivation of the puritan 'three ways' is embodied in the puritan saint who displayed features closely resembling his catholic counterpart (ch. 7).

The meditative tradition after 1650 was marked chiefly by greater ascetical rigours on the one hand, and a tendency to simplify the 'art' on the other. Also, the Ignatian and Salesian strains became noticeable. Behind these developments were not only the concern for spiritual proficiency but also the challenge of enthusiasm (ch. 8). What is distinctive about enthusiasm is that the Spirit became a practical option for the Christian life, so that the duty of meditation tended to be generalised and its contents ethicised. These processes are illustrated in the teachings of Sibbes, Cotton, Firmin, and Owen. The last-named made the most concerted attempt at resolving the tension between duty and the distinctive pneumatology of the enthusiasts, but the result is a meditation stripped of much of its ascetical characteristics.

55 The challenge of transformation: towards a theology of work in the light of the thought of H. Richard Niebuhr

Gibbs, J.R. *Cambridge* Ph.D. 1990.

This dissertation undertaken a critical analysis and development of the thought of H. Richard Niebuhr and applies it to the issue of a theology of work. A secondary goal is the reinterpretation of Niebuhr's thought, especially with regard to his understanding of God and of the Holy Spirit.

The opening chapter surveys contemporary theologies of work and identifies a number of concerns by which they have been shaped. The project of the thesis is outlined as being to integrate these concerns within an overall framework and to examine more closely than hitherto the relevance of the doctrines of God, Christ and the Holy Spirit to the issue of human work.

In Chapter Two, Niebuhr's doctrine of God is critically examined, with special attention being paid to the significance of his work on the Christian interpretation of history. His conception of God as the Creator, Governor and Redeemer who takes responsibility for the community of being is outlined as the foundation for a theology of work.

Chapter Three considers Niebuhr's understanding of Christ and the Holy Spirit, highlighting his previously neglected thinking on the Spirit. The role of Christ as paradigm, as mediator of faith and as suffering redeemer, and the work of the Spirit in the life of the believer are applied to the question of human work.

Chapter Four appropriates Niebuhr's normative understanding of human life as response to the creative, governing and redeeming action of God as a basis for integrating and exploring further the areas of concern identified in chapter one.

In Chapter Five the conclusions of the study are presented and Niebuhr's conception of God's and of humanity's responsibility for the universal community of being is proposed as the framework for a theology of work.

I am a sort of middle man: John Newton and the English evangelical tradition between the conversations of Wesley and Wilberforce

Hindmarsh, D.B. *Oxford*. D.Phil. 1993.

This thesis is a study of some aspects of the life and religious thought of John Newton (1725-1807), set in the context of English evangelicalism in c. 1740-90. Its central themes are Newton's spirituality, theology and ministry. The argument is advanced that Newton represented a median position within the evangelical tradition during his lifetime. His spirituality emphasized conversion as both a crisis and an ongoing experience of transformation; his theology sought to avoid extremes of legalism and antinomianism; and his pastoral practice and understanding of church order reflected a compromise between high views of either Church or Dissent.

The Chapters proceed in a roughly chronological pattern through Newton's life, but the method followed is that of exposition and analysis of key themes, rather than of biography in the sense of a connected chronological narrative. The subjects treated are as follows: Newton's spiritual autobiography; his theological formation and adoption of Calvinistic beliefs; his ordination; the nature and limits of his Calvinism; his ministry at Olney; his private devotion and his practice of spiritual direction; and, finally, his ministry in London and his ecclesiology.

This thesis concludes that, because of his catholicity, Newton's biography illuminates several important features of evangelicalism during his lifetime. Evangelicals were bound together by belief in a transforming, divinely revealed gospel, accessible to all. In contrast, matters of church order and distinctive points of confessional belief tended to divide them. Newton sought chiefly to preserve an understanding of the gospel that would stimulate and express the experience of conversion which was central to his own religious identity.

Interdependence of law and grace in John Wesley's teaching and preaching

Tyson, J.H. *Edinburgh*. PhD. 1992.

The purpose of this study is to prove that from 1738, in Wesley's preaching and teaching, both law and grace are proclaimed and function together in strict interdependence. Wesley firmly resisted all attempt to disrupt the delicate theological balance between these two elements. In exploring this idea, we will first trace the formation of Wesley's theology of law and grace, through the moralistic influence of the Church of England and the evangelical influence of the Moravians. Then we will examine the controversies which help illustrate the interdependence of law and grace, as well as the boundaries of each, in Wesley's thinking.

We shall see that Wesley's doctrine of the moral law is dependant upon grace in that the desire and ability to fulfill the law comes only by the grace of faith. Wesley's doctrine of grace is dependant upon the law in that faith can be maintained and strengthened only through obedience, and in that without obedience to the moral law the fruits and purpose of grace are made void. Without Wesley's doctrine of grace, his doctrine of law is mere legalism. Yet without the law his doctrine of grace is utterly frustrated, since the ultimate purpose of grace in Wesley's thinking is to make possible that sanctification which is the fulfilling of the law.

The contention of this thesis, however, is not merely that Wesley's doctrines of law and grace are interdependent, but that they are strictly interdependent. By strictly interdependent I mean that this interdependence is precisely defined at certain key points, and that these key points of interdependence remain constant without exception from 1738.

The purpose of stating the faith: a historical and systematic inquiry into the tradition of fundamental articles with special reference to Anglicanism

Pickard, S. *Durham*. PhD.

Stating the faith in the form of fundamental articles has, historically, provided an important strategy by which the identity and continually of the church has been expressed. The issue underlying this ecclesiological context of fundamental articles concerns the truth of the one-in-Christ bond in Christianity. However, discussion of fundamental articles of the faith has, from the Post-Reformation period, tended to occur as somewhat disconnected from wider concerns to do with the belief, discipleship and mission of the Church. One result is Christianity remain undisclosed and undeveloped.

By means of a multi-level approach-contemporary relevance (Part One), historical development (Part Two), case studies (Part Three) and systematic inquiry (Part Four) - this thesis develops an understanding of fundamental articles which shows how the theme is enmeshed within and contributes to the dynamic of

Christian faith in the Church. The resources for this inquiry are drawn from an extensive, but hitherto largely unexamined treatment, of the theme of fundamental articles in Anglicanism.

The Protestantism tradition of speaking about fundamental articles of faith is found to offer an important medium through which the reality of being one-in-Christ can be identified, communicated and strengthened. In this way the tradition proves a valuable means for uncovering and examination the purpose(s) of stating the faith. The problematic role of fundamental articles in Anglican self-understanding reveals itself as an instance of a more general, controversial and unfinished task in theology to state the truth of God's creating and redeeming love.

The thesis thus draws attention to the significance of fundamental articles for expressing the nature and form of ecclesiastical faith and discipleship. A positive rationale emerges for a more intensive and discerning engagement with the fundamental articles tradition as a strategy by which theology can serve the mission of the Church.

59. Jewish mission in the Christian state: Protestant missions to the Jews in 18th and 19th century Prussia

Clark, C.M. *Cambridge.* PhD. 1991.

The Institutum Judaicum in Halle, established by the Pietist Johann Heinrich Callenberg in 1728, was the first organised attempt by Protestants to missionize among the Jews. It printed conversionary texts, trained missionaries and sent them out to the Jewish communities of Central Europe and beyond. In 1972, the Institutum was dissolved by royal decree, but missionary activity was later resumed in Prussia when a group of influential nobles and senior bureaucrats founded the Berlin Society for the Promotion of Christianity among the Jews in 1822. This organization continued to function - amidst a network of auxiliaries and sister-societies - throughout the 19th century.

This dissertation represents the first attempt to place Prussian Jewish missionary activity in its political and social context. It examines the activities and publications of the Institutum Judaicum at Halle against the background of the broader phenomenon of Pietist collusion with government in projects directed towards the cultural and social homogenisation of Brandenburg Prussia under Frederick William I. Parallels are drawn between the institute at Halle and the orphanages, poor-houses, factories and schools established by Pietists and others in early 18th-century Prussia for the recuperation and rendering productive of groups which here, or threatened to become, socially marginal. Particular attention is given to the way in which the key Pietist terms 'conversion' and 'rebirth' came to refer as much to a social and occupational adjustment as to a change in belief.

19th-century missionary activity in Prussia was managed and supported by some of the most influential individuals in the kingdom. Laymen predominated, among them generals, aristocrats and senior bureaucrats. The society enjoyed the patronage and warm support of kings

Frederick William III and IV. After setting the foundation and early growth of the missionary movement against the background of the conservative religious 'Awakening' of the post-war period and charting its troubled progress through the 1830s, when 'religious association' were widely suspected of being the hot-beds for Old Lutheran separatism, the dissertation looks at ways in which the missions responded to the emancipatory liberalism which they feared would succeed in 'de-christianizing' Prussian (and German) society. It finds that in the 19th century, as in the 18th, economic, theological and social motifs were inextricably bound up in missionary accounts of the 'Jewish Question'. 'Jewish Questions' posed themselves in ways which were specific to each period, but in both the 18th and the 19th centuries, they were posited upon prior, 'Prussian Questions'.

A missionary of the road: the theology of mission and evangelism in the writings of David J. Bosch

Livingston, J.K. *Aberdeen*. PhD. 1989.

This study attempts to describe David Bosch's theology of mission and evangelism, and evaluate his contribution to the Church of South Africa and beyond.

Part One examines Bosch's historical context. Bosch's Afrikaner identity is probed, including the relationship between the Dutch Reformed Church and the ideology of apartheid. We then survey Bosch's theological pilgrimage, and outline his activities as a missiologist and churchman.

Part Two expounds Bosch's theology of mission and evangelism. We explore Bosch's theological method and his understanding of missiology as a theological discipline. We review Bosch's analysis of the contemporary missionary situation by means of three models: *mission in crisis; evangelical-ecumenical; and First World-Third World*. In each motif, Bosch seeks to discover a way forward beyond present polarizations in mission theology and practice. Bosch's biblical foundation for mission is analyzed, as well as his understanding of the meaning and relationship of evangelism, mission and church growth.

In Part Three, we interpret the structure of Bosch's thought from the theological horizon of the missionary nature of the church. Three doctrines provide a framework for interpretation: eschatology, ecclesiology and soteriology. The church is *the kingdom community*, called to act as a witness and instrument of the Kingdom. We explore the creative tension between Kingdom, church and world. The church is the *alternative community* set apart from the world and called to discipleship. She is distinct, however, precisely for the sake of the world, to exemplify Christ's new community. The church is *the reconciled and reconciling community*, embodying in her life and actions the love of God in Christ. Bosch is shown to be a 'missiologist of the road', who integrates theology and practice in a faithful, contextually- relevant way within South Africa and the global church.